Men-at-Arms • 444

# Napoleon's Mounted Chasseurs of the Imperial Guard

Ronald Pawly • Illustrated by Patrice Courcelle

*Series editor* Martin Windrow

First published in Great Britain in 2008 by Osprey Publishing
Midland House, West Way, Botley, Oxford OX2 0PH, UK
443 Park Avenue South, New York, NY 10016, USA
E-mail: **info@ospreypublishing.com**

A CIP catalogue record for this book is available from the British Library

ISBN: 978 1 84603 257 8

Edited by Martin Windrow
Page layout by Alan Hamp
Index by Glyn Sutcliffe
Typeset in Helvetica Neue and ITC New Baskerville
Originated by PPS Grasmere Ltd
Printed in China through Worldprint

08  09  10  11  12   10 9 8 7 6 5 4 3 2 1

FOR A CATALOGUE OF ALL BOOKS PUBLISHED BY
OSPREY MILITARY AND AVIATION PLEASE CONTACT:

North America
Osprey Direct, c/o Random House Distribution Center, 400 Hahn Road,
Westminster, MD 21157
Email: info@ospreydirect.com

All other regions
Osprey Direct UK, P.O. Box 140 Wellingborough, Northants, NN8 2FA, UK
Email: info@ospreydirect.co.uk

**www.ospreypublishing.com**

## Artist's note

Readers may care to note that the original paintings from which
the colour plates in this book were prepared are available for private
sale. All reproduction copyright whatsoever is retained by the
Publishers. All enquiries should be addressed to:

Patrice Courcelle,
33 avenue de Vallons, 1410 Waterloo, Belgium

The Publishers regret that they can enter into no correspondence
upon this matter.

TITLE PAGE **Mounted Chasseurs escorting the Emperor
through a damaged village. The 'Guides' ride with drawn
sabres; and note the pale deerskin breeches, which were
regulation for the escort piquets. The men serving with
these escorts were carefully selected for their ability to
withstand long distances on horseback and at high speed.
(Drawing by Job; author's collection)**

# NAPOLEON'S MOUNTED CHASSEURS OF THE IMPERIAL GUARD

## THE ORIGINS OF A LEGEND

Captain Hypolite Thomas entered the Mounted Guides of the Army of Italy on 28 July 1797, and became a *brigadier-fourrier* (quartermaster corporal) on 3 January 1800. Passing into the Mounted Chasseurs of the Consular Guard, he was promoted *maréchal-des-logis chef* (sergeant-major) in June 1801, and *adjudant sous-lieutenant* in October 1802. He was present at many major battles, rising to the rank of captain before being commissioned *major* in the 11th Line Chasseurs. Here he wears full dress, showing clearly the more elaborate braiding of his dolman and the rich light grey fur of his pelisse – the latter tended to vary according to fashion. (Private collection, France)

THE STORY OF the Mounted Chasseurs of the Imperial Guard is the story of Napoleon himself and of his campaigns, since on almost every field – from Arcole to Waterloo – he kept his 'Guides' closer to him than any other troops. (This old 1790s title survived in everyday use long after their official renaming as Mounted Chasseurs.)

In exile on St Helena, Napoleon would write that after the battle of Borghetto (30 May 1796) during his first Italian campaign, when his army were pursuing the Austrians, he felt unwell and returned to his field headquarters, where he took a warm footbath. He did not enjoy it for long, since a patrol of Austrian lancers suddenly appeared close by. Alarmed, he and his staff leapt into the saddle to flee for their lives, and he had to leave his boots and breeches behind. He wrote that it was this event that prompted him shortly afterwards to create a company of Guides to serve and guard him and his staff – and thus were born the Chasseurs à cheval de la Garde Impériale.

Like much else in Bonaparte's memoirs, this colourful anecdote is untrue, at least in its claimed consequences. In fact the commanders-in-chief of French Revolutionary armies in the field had been allowed to have a unit of so-called Guides since April 1792, and such a unit had been organized for the first Army of Italy in 1793. The only difference from the Guides of later years was that in the early 1790s they were dispersed, serving with other senior officers or guarding the paperwork of the general staff.

When Gen Bonaparte took command of the Army of Italy on 2 March 1796 his predecessor Gen Kellermann must already have had a corps of Guides, but probably this was so dispersed that it needed to be reorganized. On 24 April, Bonaparte ordered that each day a 30-strong mounted piquet, commanded by a lieutenant and a sub-lieutenant, was to serve at his field headquarters. Each time he rode out, half of them were to follow him while the rest stayed behind on guard. This order was followed on 29 May by another creating two battalions of Foot Grenadiers, and stating that these, with 50 mounted Guides, were to be available to protect the headquarters. On 2 May 1796 the Guides had been instructed to ride to Milan to be

3

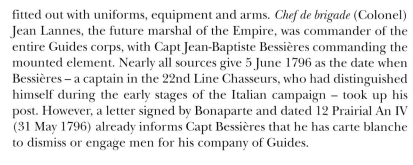

Guide of General Bonaparte during the first Italian campaign. For full dress they wore the Revolutionary hussar-style uniform with the typical mirleton headdress – scarlet with white edging, cords and flounders and a scarlet plume. The pelisse was dark blue and the breeches and dolman scarlet, all with white braiding. (Drawing by Maurice Toussaint from Marcel Dupont's *Guides de Bonaparte*)

fitted out with uniforms, equipment and arms. *Chef de brigade* (Colonel) Jean Lannes, the future marshal of the Empire, was commander of the entire Guides corps, with Capt Jean-Baptiste Bessières commanding the mounted element. Nearly all sources give 5 June 1796 as the date when Bessières – a captain in the 22nd Line Chasseurs, who had distinguished himself during the early stages of the Italian campaign – took up his post. However, a letter signed by Bonaparte and dated 12 Prairial An IV (31 May 1796) already informs Capt Bessières that he has carte blanche to dismiss or engage men for his company of Guides.

**The Italian campaign**

On 3 August 1796 the Guides saw their first action in the combat of Lonato, outside this small fortified town at the southern end of Lake Garda. Here Bonaparte struck the Austrian Gen Quosdanovic's smaller force as it marched – divided by the lake from its main body – to raise the siege of Mantua. During the battle a number of Guides were selected by Bonaparte's *aide-de-camp* Andoche Junot to make a charge against the Austrians. Junot, like Joachim Murat, was one of those officers who could achieve wonders by the sheer example of their personal élan; at Lonato he took that handful of troopers, placed himself at their head in front of the 15th Dragoons, and charged like a madman, pulling the dragoons after them. The charge was the catalyst for a French victory that brought them several thousand prisoners and 20 guns. This debut was followed by further interventions on Italian battlefields, and on each occasion the Guides covered themselves with glory. On the evening after the battle of Rovereto on 4 September, Bessières was promoted to *chef d'escadron* (squadron-leader) for his participation in this action; he had successfully charged, again with only a handful of Guides, an Austrian gun battery that was trying to flee the field. They were not always so lucky; in the engagement at Bassano on 6 November they lost two Guides killed and Lt Guérin wounded.

The Guides received their first regulated organization on 25 September 1796. They now numbered 1 squadron-leader (Bessières), 1 captain, 1 lieutenant, 2 sub-lieutenants, 1 sergeant-major, 6 sergeants, 8 corporals, 136 troopers, 1 veterinary, 2 farriers, 1 saddler and 2 *bourreliers* (leather-workers – i.e. harness-makers). They were also allowed to have a band, for which the sum of 1,200 francs was reserved, and a four-horse wagon to carry their equipment. To fill the gaps in the ranks, Bonaparte ordered that every cavalry regiment in the Army of Italy should send a number of troopers to the Guides (not a popular order with their colonels). Steadily the corps increased in size and in capability; by 30 May 1797, like the infantry of Bonaparte's Corps of Guides, they had even received two 8-pounder guns of a mounted battery, manned by 26 officers and men.

On 15–17 November 1796 the French Army of Italy, with 20,000 men, met a new Austrian army under Baron Allvintzy, 60,000 strong, at Arcole, and a three-day battle on the banks of the Adige river followed. With mobility limited to the few raised dykes which crossed the flooded rice-fields it proved impossible to force the Austrian positions, while the single bridge was stubbornly held by an Austrian Grenzer battalion. Bonaparte urgently needed to regain the initiative; he turned to *Chef d'escadrons* Bessières, and told him to pick an energetic officer and 25 troopers of his Guides. Bessières chose Lt 'Hercule', an African in the service of the Republic; he instructed him to follow the Adige for half a mile, and then to make a surprise attack on the enemy's rear. Hercule succeeded in getting behind enemy lines, where he ordered the charge, with loud shouts of *'Vive la Nation!'* and Trumpeter Bonnet blowing fit to crack his cheeks. The little company made enough noise for half a regiment, and the Austrians, taken completely by surprise, did not react before the Guides were amongst their ranks, sabring right and left. This brief shock gave Bonaparte his moment; he renewed the attack, forced his way across the bridge, and eventually secured a French victory.

On 20 December 1796 Bonaparte's chief-of-staff, Gen Louis-Alexandre Berthier, informed Bessières that Hercule had been promoted captain in the Guides, and asked the squadron-leader to provide the names of the troopers who had ridden with him; they were to receive a grant of 72 francs each. Hercule in fact received 5,000 francs and an engraved 'sabre of honour', while his comrades divided 20,000 francs between them, and Bonnet was promoted to trumpet-corporal. By now the Guides were a well-known and respected unit in the army, and Bessières himself was promoted *chef de brigade* on 9 March 1797.

On 22 December 1797 the chief-of-staff *ad interim* of the Army of Italy ordered Bessières, who was with his Guides at Monza, to lead them back to France and await further orders when they reached Fontainebleau. The next day Bessières received a letter from Gen Berthier ordering him to join the army that the French were concentrating near the Channel. Berthier advised the commander of the Guides to tell his men that they had earned universal admiration and esteem for their military accomplishments and patriotism; but that they still had to demonstrate one further quality in order to merit this admiration, a quality that would distinguish soldiers who fought for liberty and for only one master. They now had to march across allied territories and French soil; they must prove themselves by respecting the countryside, the citizens and their property. What Berthier meant was that they had to show themselves worthy to be the Guides of General Bonaparte; his letter shows clearly that an *ésprit de corps* and a unquestioning loyalty to Bonaparte were consciously being created.

## Egypt

With peace on the Continent restored, the only active enemy of the Republic was Great Britain. The members of the Directory – the Revolutionary regime then ruling France – were well aware of the growing popularity of the dashing Gen Bonaparte, the hero of the Italian campaign who had brought France a necessary and victorious peace. Bonaparte, on the other hand, felt that he could use more victories to strengthen his position still further – so both parties had their reasons for seeking another theatre of war, and Egypt suited them best. Bonaparte saw it as a chance to disrupt Britain's vital trading links with the East, and his government saw it as an opportunity to get a dangerously popular general well away from France.

When he sailed from Toulon for Egypt on 19 May 1798 aboard the French flagship *L'Orient*, Bonaparte took with him his Foot and Mounted Guides as well as the small artillery element. The Mounted

The Revue de Quintidi – a study by two master painters, Vernet and Isabey (the latter for the portraiture), shows on the left Eugène de Beauharnais, stepson of Napoleon, as commander of the Mounted Chasseurs in c.1800. After returning from Egypt the Guides had adopted the black fur colback or busby. Eugène wears full dress, with an elaborate gold-embroidered pouch belt and saddlecloth as befitting his exalted place in Bonaparte's service. The aiguillettes were a distinction of the Consular Guard; the expensive white heron plume identified superior officers (i.e. those of field rank) – the squadron officer next to him has the unit's standard red-over-green plume.

Guides already enjoyed a privileged status, since they served on board ship as the bodyguard to the general and his staff, while the others had to help in working the ship.

Once in Alexandria, on 6 July 1798 Gen Bonaparte reorganized his Corps of Guides into ten companies: five Mounted, of which one was auxiliary, and five Foot companies, of which two were auxiliaries. In addition there were 60 gunners for the artillery, a staff, and 20 musicians – in all, 1,244 men. As in Italy, the soldiers were drawn from the other regiments of the Army of the Orient, and a 'reserve Guard' was created. The Mounted Guides' staff now consisted of a *chef de brigade* and 2 squadron-leaders; the five companies each had 1 captain, 1 lieutenant, 2 sub-lieutenants, and 112 NCOs, troopers and trumpeters. The Line regiments were still naturally reluctant to provide the corps with their best soldiers, and it would be several months before the Corps of Guides was fully organized. One of the most promising newcomers during the Egyptian campaign was Gen Bonaparte's stepson Eugène de Beauharnais, who served as an ADC to the commander-in-chief. Entering the Guides, this young man would soon become close friends with his commander, Col Bessières.

For these French troops Egypt must have been a hell on earth; in extreme summer temperatures, and ravaged by diseases (including bubonic plague), they had to march immense distances across the inhospitable desert. The Guides served with distinction, as usual, following their commander-in-chief everywhere he went. At Mount Tabor on 16 April 1799, during Bonaparte's siege of St Jean-d'Acre, Gen Kléber's division, some 3,000-strong and standing in square formation, resisted a Turkish army alone for about ten hours before Bonaparte came to their help. The four companies of Mounted Guides that had followed him were ordered to charge, and again succeeded in creating a shockwave of confusion within the enemy's ranks.

The campaigns in Upper Egypt and Syria against Egyptian and Turkish armies swung one way and then the other. No final decision seemed imminent and – cut off from reinforcement since Adm Nelson's destruction of his fleet at Aboukir Bay in August 1798 – Bonaparte was frustrated by news of Russian and Austrian successes back in Europe. In June 1799 he decided that he could not stay in Egypt; his destiny lay in France, where the political and military situation had deteriorated seriously. After a last victory over the Turks at Aboukir on 25 July, a month later Bonaparte secretly slipped away, leaving his army in Kléber's hands as he sailed for home. The Corps des Guides d'Etat-major ('...of the General Staff'), more than 1,000 strong, were left behind with the rest of his army; they continued to serve under the successive commanders-in-chief – Gens Kléber and Menou – until the latter's final surrender to the British on 30 August 1801.

Bonaparte took home with him only 112 Mounted and 120 Foot Guides, chosen for their long service and loyalty. On 16 October 1799 he arrived in Paris; and there, three weeks later on 18 Brumaire (9/10 November), he took power in a coup d'état, establishing the Consulate regime with himself as First Consul.

## THE CONSULAR GUARD

On 28 November 1799 the newly created First Consul ordered the organization of a Consular Guard. This was based on the troops already serving in the Garde du Directoire, which had no light cavalry component; it comprised a staff, two battalions of Foot Grenadiers and two squadrons of Mounted Grenadiers. Now Bonaparte called for his Guides; commanded by Capt AdjMaj Dahlmann, these were still waiting for orders near Valence in the south of France. But things did not go as quickly as the First Consul wished: on 25 and 26 December 1799 he complained to the Minister of War that the Guard had not yet been fully organized. His Guides had arrived in Paris to serve with the Consular Guard on 17 December, and eight days later they had not yet received new uniforms or horses. The impatient Bonaparte returned the Minister of War's plan for the new Guard, with the opinion that it was too big: two Foot Grenadier battalions, one company of Foot Chasseurs, one squadron each of Mounted Grenadiers and Light Horse and an artillery company – in all, a maximum of 2,100 men – would be enough for the time being.

On 3 January 1800 a new organization was decreed. Alongside the two squadrons of Mounted Grenadiers a company of Mounted Chasseurs was created, numbering 4 officers and 113 troopers. Eugène de Beauharnais, aged just 19 and a captain for only two weeks, became its commander. Most of the rank-and-file were chosen from the Mounted Guides who had returned with Bonaparte from Egypt – the majority of them also being veterans of the Guides of the Army of Italy. Their long and devoted service to the person of Bonaparte would elevate this tiny unit to become the élite within the Consular Guard; officially titled the Mounted Chasseurs, they would also keep their more popular name of 'Guides' in memory of their origins. The foundations for the future Chasseurs à cheval de la Garde Impériale had been laid.

By early May 1800, dressed in their new uniforms and commanded by Eugène, they left Paris for a second Italian campaign, crossing the Alps by the St Bernard Pass. For the first time the Consular Guard, with Bessières as commander of its cavalry, would serve together as a unified formation. At the battle of Marengo on 14 June 1800 the 'Guides' were severely tested; of the 115 horses present on the strength at the start of the battle, only 45 were left at the end of that day. One thing was confirmed, however: the Consular Guard was a homogeneous élite reserve corps within the army. On 22 June part of the Consular Guard left Milan to carry the enemy regimental standards captured at Marengo back in triumph to Paris, where they arrived on 14 July. For his service at Marengo, Eugène was promoted to squadron-leader, and his unit was enlarged on 8 September to a two-company squadron, each with 1 captain, 3 lieutenants and 117 NCOs, troopers and trumpeters.

Between 1775 and 1808 the Hessian artist Nicolas Hoffmann lived in Paris, where he depicted many troops. In December 1804 he painted the Line and Guard units present for the coronation of Napoleon, and his studies show several details we would not expect to see at this date. Here Prince Eugène (right) is surrounded by his officers, all in full dress. Eugène's heavily embroidered sabretache with the Consular arms is visible, as are the panther-skin saddle and holster-covers edged with gold braid, scarlet piping, and an outer 'ruffled' edging of dark green. Both Eugène and the officer at left have the white heron plumes of field officers – is the latter *Major* Morland? (Anne S.K. Brown Collection, Providence, USA)

Recognizing the importance of having a loyal élite force of light cavalry under his hand, the First Consul added a second squadron on 6 August 1801; each now had a staff of 1 squadron-leader, 1 adjutant-major, 2 adjutant sub-lieutenants, 2 standard-bearers, 1 trumpet-corporal, 1 master tailor, 1 master bootmaker, 1 master saddler and 1 master armourer-spurrier (*armurier-éperonnier*). The two companies of each squadron each had 1 captain, 1 first-lieutenant, 1 second-lieutenant, 1 sub-lieutenant, 1 sergeant-major, 4 sergeants, 1 quartermaster, 8 corporals, 96 Chasseurs, 1 farrier and 2 trumpeters, totalling 117 men for each company – with 36 stableboys to take care of their horses!

In late September 1801 the surviving Guides who had returned from Egypt with the remnants of the Army of the Orient were admitted into the Mounted Chasseurs of the Consular Guard. A report of 10 October on the organization of the cavalry of the Consular Guard mentions that it consists of a staff, three squadrons of Mounted Grenadiers and two of Mounted Chasseurs, totalling 1,236 men with 1,251 horses.

Nearly a month later, on 14 November, the Mounted Chasseurs received regimental status (while retaining an actual strength of two squadrons), to be commanded by a *chef de brigade*. The First Consul reserved the right to nominate personally the commander of the regiment, but for the time being he kept his stepson in this post. The 1st Squadron was commanded by Eugène with captains Beurmann and Triaire as company commanders, and the 2nd by the famous Hercule, with captains Delacroix and Dominique.

On 8 March 1802, during the reorganization of the Guard, the Mounted Chasseurs still numbered two squadrons but the regimental staff was augmented: two more standard-bearers were appointed, bringing the total to four – one for each company; there would now be a trumpet-major and 2 trumpet-corporals instead of 1, plus a horse-drummer. Later that year, on 1 October, the regiment was raised to a strength of four squadrons, now totalling 56 officers and 959 men. Twelve days later Eugène was finally promoted *chef de brigade*. His squadron leaders were Morland, Dahlmann, Beurmann and Hercule.

On 21 January 1804 more changes were introduced. Squadron-leader Morland became the regiment's *major* (an appointment, not a rank) with the rank of a colonel in the Line. The Mamelukes became part of the Mounted Chasseurs; and it was ordered that the squadron-leaders were to be rotated so that they did not have the same squadron permanently under their command.[1]

Since they served as the personal guard of the First Consul, Bessières always insisted that his unit ranked above all others in the army, not only in function, bravery and honour but also in the quality and splendour of their uniforms. An army that spent most of its time on campaign naturally wore all sorts of uniform combinations, but he insisted that his Mounted Chasseurs show a religious respect for theirs.

# THE IMPERIAL GUARD

On 18 May 1804 the order of the day announced that 'Today, the Guard takes the title of Imperial Guard'. The next day at 1.30pm its officers went to the palace of Saint-Cloud to present themselves to the newly created Emperor; and at 4.30pm the Imperial Guard gathered on the Champ de Mars to be sworn in. A month later, on 29 July 1804, the Guard's new organization was decreed. For the Mounted Chasseurs there was an increase of regimental staff and company officers, raising regimental strength to 1,018 sabres. With the new status, one of the first changes to the uniforms was the adoption of buttons embossed with the crowned eagle. The actual Imperial crown would not be the only one that the Emperor settled on his own head; by also crowning himself with the Iron Crown of Charlemagne on 26 May 1805, the Emperor of the French became simultaneously the King of Italy. To assist in these ceremonies a large detachment of the Imperial Guard, of which Eugène commanded two squadrons of Mounted Chasseurs and the Mamelukes, had been ordered to march towards Italy. He would write almost daily to his friend Bessières; his letter of 3 February 1805 complained that the only troops he had problems with were the Mamelukes, who were 'fit only for parades'. First they became very miserable when it rained, then they had problems climbing or descending mountains, and they were always injuring their horses; they suffered so much that they hindered the march of the rest of the troops. On 17 February, Eugène was in Lyon and with him 20 officers of the Mounted Chasseurs with 293 troopers, and 13 more unfit for service; the Mamelukes numbered 8 officers with 75 troopers, and had 8 men unfit.

Eugène was promoted to *général de brigade* on 6 March 1805, and immediately to *général de division* a few days later; on 13 May he was created Viceroy of Italy. While he retained his nominal command of

---

1  See Men-at-Arms 429, *Napoleon's Mamelukes*

the Mounted Chasseurs, during his lengthy stays in Italy the everyday command of the unit passed to Col Morland, second in command, while Dahlmann became the major. On 13 July 1805 the Mounted Chasseurs returned to France, arriving in Paris after a 32-day march.

After nine years the Mounted Chasseurs of the Imperial Guard had reached their final establishment and organization, which would see only minor changes during the rest of the regiment's existence. They also retained much of their former uniforms. In the early days one could describe these as a long-tailed dark green *habit* coat with a scarlet collar, pointed green lapels and cuffs, and red piping; dark green trousers; and a red waistcoat with two rows of brass buttons. They had double aiguillettes to the left shoulder, and a trefoil shoulder knot to the right, in *aurore* ('dawn' – a pinkish-orange colour). Their headdress was at first a felt bicorn hat worn *'en colonne'* (fore-and-aft), with a tall red-over-green plume. On their return from Egypt they had adopted the black fur colback or busby with a similar plume; they kept the bicorn for *tenue ordinaire* and *tenue de ville*, but the colback became their distinctive headgear. Later, the waistcoat with a double row of buttons was kept only for the *petite tenue;* the full dress waistcoat was equally scarlet, but with a single row of buttons and *aurore* braiding.

On 28 August 1805, from the Camp de Boulogne beside the English Channel, Napoleon ordered Marshal Berthier to have the Imperial Guard leave their quarters and march for Strasbourg. Two days later Eugène, still in Italy but aware of the imminent campaign against Austria, advised Bessières to use the *petite tenue* when his men went on campaign, as he thought this was the most handsome *'uniforme de guerre'* they had. Riding off eastwards, the Mounted Chasseurs of the Guard were organized into a brigade of two tactical *régiments de marches* each of three squadrons, plus the Mamelukes. The regimental staff, which rode with the 1st Marching Regiment, comprised 2nd Col Morland, Sub-AdjMaj Domangé, the paymaster Delassus and one medical officer – 4 officers and their 10 horses, plus 2 troopers with 2 horses.

The 1st Marching Regiment comprised the 1st Squadron (commanded by SqnLdrs Bourbier and Clerc, with 2 captains, 2 first-lieutenants and 2 second-lieutenants); the 2nd Sqn (SqnLdr Beurmann plus 1 captain, 3 first-lieutenants and 3 second-lieutenants); and the 3rd Sqn (SqnLdr Guyot plus 1 captain, 3 first-lieutenants and 3 second-lieutenants). This marching regiment totalled 24 officers with 62 horses, and 365 rank-and-file with 356 horses.

The staff of the 2nd Marching Regt in the brigade was led by its commanding officer Maj Dahlmann, with Sub-AdjMaj Mexner plus a trooper – 2 officers with 9 horses, plus the lone Chasseur with his horse. The regiment itself was composed of the 4th Sqn (SqnLdr Charpentier assisted by 2 captains, 2 first-lieutenants and 3 second-lieutenants); the 5th Sqn (SqnLdr Bohn

Trooper of the Mounted Chasseurs of the Guard in full dress, by Hoffmann. Even though this was painted in 1804–05 he still has the old Consular arms on his sabretache, and scarlet breeches (see Plates B1 & B2). These would soon be replaced with green breeches, and a sabretache showing the Imperial arms. (Ann S.K. Brown Collection, Providence, USA)

with 1 captain, 3 first-lieutenants and 3 second-lieutenants); and the 6th Sqn (SqnLdr Thiry with 1 captain, 2 first-lieutenants and 3 second-lieutenants). The regimental strength was 23 officers with 57 horses, and 363 rank-and-file with 352 horses. The entire Chasseur brigade stood at 6 staff and 47 regimental officers with 138 horses, and 731 enlisted men with 711 horses. There was in fact a shortfall of only 12 troop horses – some of the troopers were assigned to drive wagons, so the shortage was less than it appears. The brigade was followed by a number of support vehicles including, for example, 6 ammunition caissons and a field forge. The accompanying Mamelukes, commanded by Capt Delaître, had a strength of 6 officers with their 13 horses and 71 Mamelukes each with one horse.

### The Vélites

While the Guard cavalry rode off to new victories, the Emperor decreed on 19 September 1805 the creation of a Corps of Mounted *Vélites* – an almost untranslatable term, meaning young volunteers from the moneyed classes whose families actually paid for them to serve. The corps was to be about 800 strong, in two large squadrons of four companies, each company with 119 sabres. The Mounted Grenadiers and Chasseurs were each assigned one squadron, and detachments from these were sent on campaign to be divided between the other squadrons in their respective regiments, in order to bring their company strengths up to 125 enlisted men. The remaining Vélites would form a 5th Squadron for each regiment, and with this augmentation each regiment would number some 1,400 men.

Not everyone was happy with this decision; the officers and soldiers of the Guard had to qualify by the necessary years of service and minimum number of campaigns for entry into this élite corps, while these Vélites only had to meet the physical requirements and to have parents able to pay an allowance for the privilege. Some officers even warned the Emperor that when he was with the army or in Paris they would prefer to see him surrounded by veteran soldiers of the Guard undiluted by these johnnies-come-lately who had not proved their loyalty in battle. Each department (administrative region) had to provide six of these volunteers, taken from the last three annual conscription classes; if there were not enough volunteers then the departmental prefect was to select men. In fact the idea was an immediate success, since young men of means and education were much keener to serve in this élite corps than somewhere in a Line regiment, and in no time all the vacancies were taken up.

Eugène de Beauharnais in full dress, painted by Henry Scheffer as a general, an Imperial prince, and colonel-in-chief of the Mounted Chasseurs. Eugène's dolman, its sleeves covered to the elbow with gold rank braiding, has a red collar, unlike those worn by his regiment; note too the details of the panther-skin saddle cover over a second shabraque. It is interesting that his harness is of plain leather, like any trooper's. He wears the sash of the Grand Cross of the Legion of Honour over his dolman and the star on his pelisse.

# THE EARLY CAMPAIGNS

## 1805: The pursuit from Ulm

In late September 1805, marching via Strasbourg, the Mounted Chasseurs entered Germany, while a handful of them were selected to fulfil escort duties for the Emperor. As support, five guns (3x 8-pdrs and 2x 4-pdrs) together with 12 caissons were attached to the regiment, as well as a spare limber, a field forge, a wagon and an ammunition cart. On 9 October they crossed the River Danube. Once in contact with the enemy the cavalry of the Guard, commanded by Marshal Bessières, supported the Line cavalry when required. The French advance was so fast that they were able to encircle the whole army of the lethargic Gen von Mack, concentrated at Ulm.

The unfortunate Mack surrendered on 15 October; and the following evening the Mounted Chasseurs arrived at a village reserved for the Emperor's headquarters. In pouring rain they started looking for shelter, occupying houses reserved for the Emperor's household; when the latter arrived, they were rather brutally refused access. The next day part of the Austrian army, under Archduke Ferdinand, was reported to have escaped from the Ulm encirclement; hearing this, Napoleon ordered Marshal Murat to hunt them down. To punish his Mounted Chasseurs for their arrogant behaviour the night before, he suspended the regiment from all their normal duties and ordered Murat to put them in the vanguard of his cavalry corps. The imperial instructions were simple: 'Do not spare them, and keep them in the vanguard as long you are chasing the Austrians.' For 12 long days the weary Chasseurs would be in the saddle night and day, but in the process they would more than redeem their reputation. They were soon on the heels of the fleeing Austrians, and eventually two-thirds of the troops who had escaped encirclement in Ulm were captured, together with 50 guns and 18 colours and standards.

When Hoffmann painted this series of illustrations the Chasseurs' uniforms were still in transition between Consular and Imperial styles; this trumpeter still has the Consular arms on his crimson-faced sabretache. His colback is white, with a unique white-over-crimson plume; his dolman is sky-blue, the pelisse crimson with black fur, and the breeches crimson. The crimson saddle cloth shows a line of gold chain embroidery inside the edging braid. (Ann S.K. Brown Collection, Providence, USA)

On 21 October the retreating Austrians were sighted near Nuremberg and Murat's spearpoint, consisting of Lt Desmichel's 30-odd Chasseurs, came up against about 300 Austrian light infantry covering the retreat. The Mounted Chasseurs threw themselves on this demoralized rearguard with the sabre, and in minutes they surrendered, to be taken back to the rest of Desmichel's squadron following at a distance. With this formality completed the chase resumed, and a few hundred yards further on Desmichel spotted more prey – another 400 infantrymen. Once contact was made these too threw down their weapons and surrendered, leaving two colours in Desmichel's hands.

Nothing could stop the Chasseurs now, and yet again they drove ahead. This time they found Austrian cavalry marching along a sunken road; hearing gunfire from their infantry, some 500 dragoons from the Latour Regiment had made an about-turn to come to their aid. Desmichel's handful of men was by now reduced to about 24, the rest wounded and left behind; nevertheless, taking advantage of the narrow sunken road, Desmichel charged. Unable to see the numbers opposing them, the Austrians flinched under the shock; uncertain and surprised by this vigorous attack, they fell or fled one by one, retreating in haste. They left behind them 50 dead, some 150 prisoners (including the regiment's colonel and a number of his officers), 25 guns, and all their baggage and wagons. On 22 October the Mounted Chasseurs' actions were mentioned in the 10th Bulletin of the Grande Armée. A week later they returned to the Imperial headquarters, where they resumed their service as personal bodyguard and escort to the Emperor. Desmichel was commissioned captain, and decorated with the cross of an Officer in the Legion of Honour. In five days the cavalry had covered 130 miles in pursuit of Archduke Ferdinand's troops; Murat reported to the Emperor that '12,000 prisoners of war are taken, together with two lieutenant-generals, seven major-generals and more than 200 officers; 120 guns and 500 ammunition and baggage wagons, including those of Prince Ferdinand; 11 regimental flags were taken, as well as 400,000 florins from the treasury of the Austrian corps; 800 French soldiers who had been taken by the enemy were also liberated.'

At Olmütz, on 20 November, Bessières with the Guard cavalry division assisted Murat to clear the road to Brno, which was blocked by some 6,000 Russian cavalry. Bessières brought his troops forward in two lines, the first of five squadrons – three of Mounted Grenadiers and two of Mounted Chasseurs; the second line comprised two squadrons of Mounted Grenadiers and three of Mounted Chasseurs. Taking the lead, Bessières charged the Russian cavalry with such vigour that in a few minutes the latter were in full retreat, and due to the speed of the French success they were unable to take their artillery off the field.

## Austerlitz

It was only when they reached Brno that the Guard cavalry got a few days of desperately needed rest. They left the town on 29 November; 72 hours later, the Emperors of Russia, Austria and France met on the battlefield of Austerlitz. The Grande Armée numbered about 50,000 foot and 15,000 horse, with 282 guns; the Austro-Russian armies, under the Russian Marshal Kutuzov, had about 70,000 infantry and 16,500 cavalry, with 252 guns.

The armies had taken up their positions in icy cold, and the morning of 2 December was foggy; they faced each other in lines deployed roughly north to south, the French facing east, the allies west. Napoleon knew that the allies – who should have fought a defensive battle – would attack him. The Austro-Russian left and centre were drawn up along the low hills of the Pratzen Heights, with a reserve behind their right (northern) flank; Napoleon faced them with all his weight on his left. The allies were uncertain of the exact French dispositions, but planned to attack Napoleon with their left and centre, swinging their line like a door into his right flank while their right-wing corps punched forward to dislodge his left. Their command and control were inevitably confused; this was a multi-national, multi-language force, led by proud and touchy aristocrats, and Russian staffwork in particular had a poor reputation.

The Emperor used modest forces to hold off the initial allied attacks on his right (southern) wing; he then launched Marshal Soult's infantry in a frontal attack on the Austro-Russian centre on the Pratzen plateau, to cut the over-extended allied army in two. Kutuzov sent more infantry forward in the centre, and a desperate firefight developed; meanwhile

In 1810 the German brothers Henschel published 12 plates on the French army, one of them this Mounted Chasseur in *grande tenue ordinaire* uniform. Note that they depict him with the bayonet fixed to his carbine; this was normal procedure when the escort piquet dismounted to protect the Emperor. See Plate C3 for details of this uniform, and note the *aurore* braiding on his *gilet à la hussarde*.

there was another massive clash – mostly between cavalry – to the north of the heights, in which Lannes and Murat were eventually successful in pushing Prince Bagration back. The allies' only available reserve – the Grand Duke Constantine's Russian Imperial Guard – then advanced against Soult's left flank on the Pratzen plateau.

After sucessfully holding an infantry attack, Gen Vandamme's division was driven back in ruin by charges of the Russian Guard Hussars and Horse Guard cuirassiers. Bessières, standing next to Napoleon, remarked that the fleeing French infantry were not looking backwards during their retreat, which meant that they were being pursued by cavalry. The Emperor turned to his ADC Gen Rapp, and ordered him to take two squadrons each of the Mounted Grenadiers and Mounted Chasseurs of the Guard to check the Russian advance. Rapp rode over and ordered the first two squadrons of each regiment, plus the Mamelukes, to follow him. Putting himself at their head, Rapp placed the Mounted Grenadiers to the left of the Chasseurs.

By now the advancing Russian cavalry had lost their formations, becoming increasingly dispersed in an infantry/cavalry mêlée. Rapp's charge burst upon them, with the Mounted Chasseurs ahead and the Mounted Grenadiers following. A Russian Guard artillery battery received the French horsemen with a murderous salvo, emptying many saddles – including those of Col Morland, who was mortally wounded, and Capt AdjMaj Therwey – but the Mounted Chasseurs still reached the guns, sabring the crews and capturing their pieces. Prince Repnin's aristocratic Russian Chevalier Guards were now thrown into the fighting; and Bessières, leaving one squadron of each Guard cavalry regiment with the Emperor, brought the other four squadrons into battle. The Mounted Chasseurs charged for a third time; Gen Rapp, blinded by the blood from a face wound, was rescued by Lt Chaïm of the Mamelukes. Squadron-Leader Daumesnil, surrounded by seven or eight Chevalier Guards, was also wounded and likely to be killed or taken; he was saved by the courage of the regiment's Trumpet-Major Krettly, laying about him with the *sabre d'honneur* that he had already received for saving the life of Maj Dahlmann.

While the opposing cavalry were locked in chaotic combat, Gen Drouet's French infantry division came up from Rapp's right rear, and these nine battalions provided their cavalry comrades with a base of firepower behind which to regroup before returning to the frey. The Chevalier Guards were defeated with shocking losses, and Prince Repnin was captured. As the Russian Guard cavalry were forced to fall back they exposed their infantry, obliging these regiments to form squares and retreat themselves; they were only saved from a worse slaughter by the protection of hovering Guard Hussars and some Austrian cuirassiers.

The victory – which many judge as the finest of Napoleon's career – was now assured. In the gathering darkness of the late afternoon the scattered remnants of the Austro-Russian army

Born in 1769, Nicolas Dahlmann entered the army as an *enfant de troupe*, and was on the pay list from 1777 onwards. As a trooper he took part in all the Revolutionary campaigns; arriving in Italy to serve under Bonaparte in 1796, he joined the Guides under Capt Bessières. During the Egyptian campaign he was promoted lieutenant, and returned to France with the rank of captain. In 1802 he became a squadron-leader in the Mounted Chasseurs, and in 1805 was appointed major. He replaced his commanding officer, Col Morland, when the latter was killed at Austerlitz. Just before the battle of Eylau, on 8 February 1807, Dahlmann was promoted general, but he asked the Emperor to allow him to lead his old regiment into that battle – where he was mortally wounded, dying two days later.

straggled away to the south and east; there was no pursuit. That night, Maj Dahlmann and two of his squadrons marched over the battlefield and gathered up another 1,500 prisoners and 20 guns. The regiment had suffered 22 killed and many more wounded. Crosses of the Legion of Honour were awarded to the survivors by the handful. Krettly, wounded several times, was commissioned a second-lieutenant, and so could send home the 'trumpet of honour' that he had received after Marengo.

* * *

Austerlitz struck a death-blow to the Third Coalition. Russia sullenly withdrew her army into her own vast territories, but Austria was immediately forced to accept humiliating peace terms. These cleared the ground for the foundation of Napoleon's puppet Confederation of the Rhine, embracing most of western and southern Germany. With the Treaty of Pressburg signed (26 December 1805), the Mounted Chasseurs returned to Paris.

A Mounted Chasseur of the Emperor's escort, by Détaille. During the 1806–07 campaigns they wore the green *habit* and braided scarlet waistcoat instead of the green dolman and scarlet pelisse. When they were not marching with drawn sabres the escort braced the carbine on the right thigh. Every time the Emperor dismounted, the escort followed his example and placed themselves in a cordon around him, with fixed bayonets. Only a restricted number of people were admitted into this protected space without asking permission from one of the ADCs or Marshal Berthier. (Army Museum, Brussels)

Major Dahlmann had taken Col Morland's place; SqnLdr Guyot, who had left the regiment earlier to organize the Corps of Vélites, became the regimental major. On 1 February 1806 the regimental personnel present at their barracks in the Paris Military School numbered 12 officers and 165 rankers, with 14 in hospital; in Milan, the Viceroy Eugène had two each of officers and troopers as members of his suite. On service with the Grande Armée were 54 officers and 791 rankers, bringing the total to 1,040 all ranks, against a normal establishment of 1,142 – the Mounted Chasseurs needed to fill 102 gaps in the ranks. Back in Paris, the regiment could enjoy the legendary status that they had won on the battlefield; they had reached not only maturity, but the pinnacle of fame within the French cavalry. The greatest honour of all was that the Emperor even wore their dark green and red undress uniform when on campaign. But the privilege of providing his personal bodyguard, ensuring his safety and escorting him everywhere he went, came at a certain price. No other regiment in the army had so many men in hospital at any one time; the unit had to provide men to fulfil these duties 24 hours a day, every day of the year, and the consequence was exhaustion, illness and accidental injuries.

The 1805 campaign – the first fought by the Imperial Guard – had proved that such a large regiment was a challenging command for a single officer. Therefore, on 15 April 1806, the Emperor added a second major to the staff, so that on campaign each *régiment de marche* could be commanded by a major. The number of squadron-leaders was increased to seven, one of them a regimental senior instructor, while the regimental staff and companies received more non-commissioned officers.

The Vélites also underwent some changes. They were now serving in a single squadron of two 125-strong companies, so that the Mounted

Chasseurs had four squadrons of Old Guard and one of Vélites. On campaign or when on a long march each squadron was to insure against casualties by enlargement to 250 men by the addition of 50 Vélites. This would bring the regimental total in the field to 1,000 rank-and-file – 800 seasoned men and 200 Vélites – while 48 Old Guard Chasseurs and 50 Vélites remained behind at the Paris depot. On 1 January 1807 those Vélites who had served during the Austerlitz campaign would be admitted into full Guard status.

### 1806: Prussia

Russia had been defeated but remained a belligerent, and in October 1806 she formed with Britain the Fourth Coalition; in this they were joined by Prussia and Saxony, both of them threatened by Napoleon's creation of the Confederation of the Rhine.

During the 1806 campaign the Mounted Chasseurs were again divided into two *régiments de marche*, this time of two squadrons each. Due to the speed with which the campaign opened on 8 October, the Mounted Chasseurs were 36 hours behind the rest of the Grande Armée's lightning advance, and were too late to be present at the battles of Jena and Auerstädt on 14 October. They arrived just in time to take back their escort duties from the 1st Hussars and to be in their rightful place around the Emperor when he entered defeated Berlin ten days later. The King of Prussia fled to Russia, and to forestall a Russian intervention Napoleon marched into Poland; on 23 November both *régiments de marche* of the Mounted Chasseurs were in Warsaw. They did not see any action in the engagements at Pultusk or Golymin (26 December), but had to endure harsh winter conditions as they provided escort piquets for the Emperor.[2] On 30 December 1806, Col Dahlmann was promoted *général de brigade*; there were no vacancies for a brigade command at that time, so he remained at the Imperial headquarters while Maj Guyot took over command of the Mounted Chasseurs.

In the snowbound Polish winter even the Guard suffered from lack of proper clothing; more than one soldier lacked a coat or cloak, and some even shoes. Napoleon ordered the mass production of all necessary equipment – for the regiment, 860 shirts, 200 greatcoats and the same number of portmanteaux. On 5 January 1807 he decreed that each of his two Guard cavalry regiments was to receive eight wagons, of which two were for the officers' portmanteaux and baggage, two for spare horse equipment and spurs, and the other four for food supplies. But provisions still remained insufficient, and by March 1807 there would be deaths from hunger in the ranks.

### 1807: Eylau

In January 1807 the Russian Gen Bennigsen advanced from the Baltic coast, and on 27 January

Mounted Chasseurs escorting a staff officer (right). The senior officer of Mounted Chasseurs (centre) wears his heavily embroidered pelisse and breeches but a plain colback; his gold-decorated red leather pouch belt would more typically be protected by a plain cover. Behind him, a trumpeter with a white colback is also wearing his pelisse, and so appears crimson from neck to knee. (Drawing by Vallet; Army Museum, Brussels)

---

2 This aspect of the regiment's duties is described in more detail in Elite 116, *Napoleon's Imperial Headquarters (2): On Campaign*

the regiment followed the Emperor north from Warsaw. The Russians fell back, and on 7 February the French caught up with them near the village of Preussisches-Eylau. The initial fighting was indecisive, since both armies were awaiting the arrival of additional forces; but on 8 February an impatient Napoleon came as close as he had ever been to outright defeat.

The regiment was placed with the Mounted Grenadiers and Mamelukes behind the Foot Guard regiments, in the left centre of the French line, on heights facing across the valley to the Russian army on high ground opposite; that day the Dragoons of the Empress were on duty near the Emperor. General Dahlmann, still without a command, asked and received permission to return to his old Mounted Chasseurs. The battlefield was covered with a thick fall of snow, and the cutting wind and iron-grey sky promised more to come. Former Trumpet-Major Krettly remembered his appearance that day: 'I wore my pelisse and had my sabre at my side. My two pistols were bound together by means of a handkerchief and slung over my waist belt. [Under my] colback ... my hair, that would normally be tied into a queue, was now hanging loose [over] my shoulders and breast. I looked very rancorous, and covered in snow, with small pearls of ice frozen in my hair.'

Napoleon had wanted to remain on the defensive on the 7th, since he was outnumbered; two of his corps – those of Ney from his left front and Davout from his right rear – were a day's march from the battlefield. They were not in sight on the morning of the 8th, when a tremendous Russian bombardment began to rake his line. Under heavy pressure on both his flanks, Napoleon ordered Augereau's VII Corps, holding his centre, to advance; but, blinded by a blizzard of snow, they lost direction and were cut to pieces by the Russian artillery. The Russian centre counter-attacked the yawning gap in the line, and soon threatened Napoleon's command post at the church in Eylau village.

In a first attempt to gain some time Napoleon ordered his duty squadron to charge, while he built up some defensive strength – his only reserves were the Guard and Murat's Reserve Cavalry Corps. The charge checked the Russian advance for a while, but the situation soon became desperate. Napoleon turned to Murat and reputedly asked him, 'Will you let us be annihilated by these people?' Murat led the entire Reserve Cavalry forward, leaving the Imperial Guard massed around Napoleon and still under heavy fire. In minutes Murat had driven back the Russian centre; but the enemy soon re-formed, leaving the Reserve Cavalry cut off from the rest of the army.

Now it was the turn of the Guard. General Dorsenne's Foot Grenadiers began to push the enemy back from the blazing village, supported by charges of the Guard cavalry. During this attack Gen Dahlmann was mortally wounded at the head of the Mounted Chasseurs. The general's nephew, Chasseur Brice, saw him fall and came to his aid; only a few yards from the fighting, Brice jumped off his horse, lifted the wounded general into his saddle and tried to lead him from the field, holding the reins in one hand and his drawn sabre in the other. A handful of Russian hussars spotted the general's gold-embroidered uniform and surrounded the pair, raining sabre cuts on Brice; his fur colback took most of them, but one left his left arm paralyzed. In the nick of time he was rescued by his squadron-mate

Chasseur Dufour, but nothing could save the life of Gen Dahlmann; his Chasseurs' only consolation was that he died in their midst rather than at the feet of the Russians.

At about noon, after some three hours' fighting, Davout's III Corps came up on Napoleon's right, but his turning of the Russian left was checked by the arrival an hour and a half later of a Prussian corps under Gen l'Estocque. Ney's VI Corps did not arrive behind the Russian right until that evening, by which time Bennigsen's army was making an orderly withdrawal. This savage battle in the snowstorm was ultimately indecisive, and very costly for both sides. The allies lost some 22,000 killed, wounded, captured and missing, and the French probably about 19,000 – well over twice the 7,500 they admitted at the time.

Immediately after the battle, trying to maintain the Emperor's invincible image, Napoleon's propaganda machine tried, in the pages of the Grande Armée's 58th Bulletin, to transform this near-disaster into a triumph of cool command. In fact the crisis of the battle had seen Napoleon forced to shelter under cover of the church while his Imperial Guard tried to save him in desperate fighting. The charge of the Guard cavalry had degenerated into a wild mêlée of broken formations. One eye-witness recalled seeing Gen Lepic, Colonel of the Mounted Grenadiers, returning from the fight in tatters; his uniform was cut to pieces, and he had left bits of his clothing and equipment – even one of his boots – on the battlefield.

Casualties were high among the Mounted Chasseurs; they lost, in addition to Gen Dahlmann, Capt Guyot (not to be confused with the regimental second-in-command), 9 NCOs and 41 rankers killed, and 15 officers, 20 NCOs and 120 Chasseurs wounded, plus more than 200 horses lost. In a letter to his Foreign Minister, Talleyrand, Napoleon wrote at 5pm on the day of the battle that his Guard cavalry had covered itself with glory, suffering only 40 killed and 150 wounded from both regiments. The Emperor's writings were consistently unreliable about such matters; he did, at least, end his letter with the words 'L'affaire a été chaude, fort animée et assez chanceuse' – 'This business was hot, very eventful, and quite chancy enough...'

Aware of what he owed his Guard cavalry, he rewarded them. On 16 February, Maj Guyot was at last commissioned colonel-major and SqnLdr Thiry replaced him as major. Pensions were granted to the families of officers killed at Eylau; an example was the father of Lt Joseph Guibert, a former standard-bearer. Reported wounded, Guibert – like so many others – died of his wounds, in his case on 12 February. His father would be granted an annual pension of 1,000 francs – a small fortune for those days.

Another of the regiment's wounded from Eylau was 21-year-old Vélite François Bertrand of the 9th Company, who lingered for many weeks but finally died on 20 April. On 6 May, SgtMaj Toulouse wrote to inform his parents of their loss. On 18 June his father received an official death certificate and a letter from the regiment's *quartier-maître* treasurer, stating that because they had given 'a defender of the state', who had died in its defence, they would be given any support needed. In July 1806 François' father had paid the allowance for his son as a Vélite: 150 francs in total, 75 francs for the period 1 April–1 July and the same amount for 1 July to 1 October 1806.

Both the French and Russian armies returned to their winter quarters, to lick their wounds and rebuild their strength for the next spring campaign. Hostilities resumed on 4 June 1807; and ten days later they met again at Friedland. Marshal Lannes' 17,000-strong Reserve Corps held off 46,000 of Bennigsen's troops who crossed the Alle river to attack them, until Napoleon could come up with twice that many and smash the Russians. The Mounted Chasseurs were not engaged in this victory.

Russia asked for an armistice on 19 June 1807, and on 9 July the Treaty of Tilsit reduced both Russia and Prussia to the status of clients of France. The Imperial Guard left for France in October, via Konigsberg and a stay in Hanover.

\* \* \*

On 25 November 1807 the Mounted Chasseurs, Fusiliers, Foot Chasseurs, Foot Grenadiers, Dragoons and Mounted Grenadiers of the Guard (in that order) entered Paris. They were still wearing their *habits de guerre*, since Napoleon – with a shrewd eye for effect – had refused to distribute new uniforms for the occasion. At the Barrière de la Villette they were received by the Mayor of Paris and the Prefect of the Department with their councils. The troops had to endure pompous speeches, but golden laurel wreaths were hung around their Eagles. All the Mounted Chasseurs squadrons were present, preceded by four standard-bearers. After the first ceremonies – and with Gen Dahlmann's black-draped coffin leading the column – the Guard paraded along the boulevards towards the Place du Carrousel in front of the Tuileries Palace, where the Emperor inspected them. Afterwards the officers were invited into the state apartments, while the regimental Eagles were taken to the Emperor's study.

The next few days would see a round of parades, receptions, banquets, balls and other festivities at which the Imperial Guard were presented as heroes. The climax was a grand ball given by Marshal Bessières, for the Guard and the leading citizens of Paris. While this was all very enjoyable, it would not last for very long; soon the Guard would be on the road once again, but first some minor changes took place. With Eugène spending much of his time in Milan as viceroy it was obvious that his colonelcy-in-chief of the Mounted Chasseurs could not continue. On 18 January, Napoleon commissioned *Général de brigade* Charles Lefebvre-Desnoëttes as the new colonel-in-chief – no doubt a disappointment for ColMaj Guyot, who had led the regiment for nearly a year.

On 1 January 1808 the regimental strength reports (not including the Mamelukes) show us that the Old Guard squadrons were quartered in Paris and the Vélites at Versailles. Present on that day were:
Old Guard: 69 officers, 944 NCOs and troopers; plus 5 officers and 40 men in hospital; total, 1,058.

Detail from a drawing by Benjamin Zix of Napoleon's meeting with the Tsar at Tilsit in July 1807. This officer of the Mounted Chasseurs wears undress, consisting of bicorn with red-over-green plume, dolman with richly embroidered rear seams, and breeches. His embroidered sabretache is clearly visible, as are the head and tail – at the rear, and extreme front – on his panther-skin saddle cover. (Collection du Musée National du Château de Malmaison)

Vélites: 10 officers, 219 NCOs and Vélites; plus 15 Vélites in hospital; total, 244.

Absentees were: With the Grande Armée, 1 officer, 4 Chasseurs and 15 Vélites; in hospitals outside France, 40 Chasseurs; total, 45 Old Guard Chasseurs and 15 Vélites.

Grand total: 1,103 Old Guard Chasseurs and 259 Vélites.

The normal establishment was 1,037 Old Guard and 312 Vélites; so the Old Guard had a surplus of 66 Chasseurs, while the Vélites were 53 men short. In the stables, 1,492 horses were counted. During the previous month, 95 new troopers with 30 horses had been admitted, while 5 troopers and 16 horses had been struck from the lists.

### 1808: Spain

One month later, on 1 February 1808, a first Guard detachment left for Bordeaux with orders to arrive on the 23rd. Riding with them were 216 Mounted Chasseurs – 12 officers, 203 NCOs and troopers – while one Chasseur was registered as 'not present'. The officers had 36 horses with them, the rank-and-file 233, plus 38 draft horses for the wagons. In his report to the Emperor, Marshal Bessières indicated that the Guard cavalry regiments (Dragoons, Grenadiers and Chasseurs) each had some 30 inexperienced soldiers still in their barracks, and asked that they should set off for Spain on 20 February. Consequently an officer of the Mounted Chasseurs left with 30 men and 40 horses to catch up with the first detachment at Bordeaux. With them rode Maj Thiry, who for the time being assumed command of the Polish Light Horse's and his own regiment's detachments.[3]

In March 1808, Marshal Murat, commander-in-chief of the troops gathered near the border with Spain, received the order to cross the Pyrenees. He took with him a detachment of Guard troops commanded by Gen Lepic, including one squadron of Mounted Chasseurs commanded by SqnLdr Daumesnil. The Mounted Chasseurs followed Murat to Madrid, where – together with the Mamelukes – they were in the thick of the city riots against the French on 2 May 1808; the casualties were SqnLdr Daumesnil, Captains Kirmann and Poiré and another 10 officers and 13 Chasseurs and Mamelukes killed or wounded.

The revolt in Madrid, and Gen Dupont's surrender of a complete corps to the Spanish at Baylen on 22 July, forced the Emperor to take personal charge of the situation. More troops of the Guard were gathered near the border; on 26 August, Gen Walther – who had temporarily taken command of the Guard in Paris while Bessières was serving in Spain – informed Napoleon that 800 Mounted Chasseurs were available for the campaign. Several detachments headed for the Pyrenees: one

In 1804 elbow-length shoulder capes were distributed to the Chasseurs for wear over the cloak, as here. The capes alone were worn when on dismounted guard duty and by the men of the escort piquets, so that everybody could identify them at a glance. This garment probably did not survive 1807, as it gave insufficient protection in foul weather. A green, sleeved *manteau-capote* with a shorter cape replaced the cloak from 1812. (Army Museum, Brussels)

---

3 For a summary of the outbreak of war in Spain and Portugal, and of the former regiment's part in it, see MAA 440, *Napoleon's Polish Lancers of the Imperial Guard.*

This drawing by Benjamin Zix shows the Mounted Chasseurs, in dolmans, parading in front of the Emperor during one of his regular reviews – on this occasion, at Schönbrunn near occupied Vienna. (Collection du Musée National du Château de Malmaison)

commanded by ColMaj Guyot on 8 October, followed on 20 October by another 325 men, raising their numbers in the field (Mamelukes included) to 1,086. With nearly the entire regiment on the march, 140 'courtes-queus' ('short-tails') of the Line were expected at the depots to fill the vacancies.[4] By then a report by Gen Lefebvre-Desnoëttes gave Imperial Guard strength as follows:

|  | In Spain | In Paris | Total |
|---|---|---|---|
| Infantry | 6,000 | 968 | 6,968 |
| Cavalry | 3,287 | 907 | 4,194 |
| Totals | 9,287 | 1,875 | 11,162 |

On 4 November the Imperial Guard, marching with Napoleon's main force, entered Spain. The next day they were at Vittoria, where Napoleon not only took command of the army but also met his brother Joseph, whom he had installed on the throne of Spain but who had been obliged to flee Madrid shortly after the defeat at Baylen. The Emperor marched on for the capital, via the pass of Somosierra, where the Mounted Chasseurs supported the Polish Lancers in their heroic charge against the Spanish defenders. Napoleon entered Madrid on 8 December 1808.

The Convention of Cintra – the instrument of the surrender, three months previously, of Gen Junot's French forces in Portugal to the British – had presented the French with shamefully generous terms for repatriation. The officers responsible, Dalrymple and Burrard, had been recalled to London to face an enquiry, and so had Sir Arthur Wellesley – the general who had actually beaten Junot, but had been superceded on the arrival of his superiors. In the meantime Sir John Moore was placed in command of the modestly reinforced British forces in Portugal, and he planned a daring strike at Marshal Soult's isolated corps on the French lines of communication. However, once in Madrid and with the security situation back under control the Emperor could turn towards Moore, who was abandoned by his Spanish allies and forced to fall back towards the embarkation ports of Vigo and Corunna. Napoleon left Madrid for the north-west on 20 December, hoping to cut the British off from their means of escape.

The conditions faced by Moore's men on this wretched retreat are well known; but the French suffered too, having to cross the 4,500-foot

---

4 By this date most regiments had abandoned long hair gathered in queues for troopers, but the Mounted Chasseurs kept the old style; most new arrivals from the ranks of Line regiments therefore had to let their hair grow before they could show off this symbol of exclusivity.

Sierra de Guadarrama in heavy snowstorms. Conditions were so bad that the cavalry were told by local inhabitants that in the past whole regiments had perished when they tried to cross the pass in such terrible weather. Time was against Napoleon, who set an example by dismounting and marching on foot followed by his staff, his Mounted Chasseurs and the rest of the army. Snow turned into rain, transforming the roads into knee-deep pools of slush and continuing to delay the advance. Knowing that the British were retreating towards the Ezla river crossing at Benavente, Napoleon ordered Gen Lefebvre-Desnoëttes to take his regiment ahead as fast as possible.

Followed by the Emperor and his staff, Lefebvre-Desnoëttes left without delay with three squadrons and some Mamelukes. His instructions were to try to delay the British retreat by any means short of a direct attack, gaining time for the army to catch up with them. After force-marching for several days the Chasseurs arrived at Benavente on 29 December, to find the bridges destroyed by the retreating British. They located a usable ford and crossed to the far bank, where British and Hanoverian rearguard cavalry were awaiting them. With an over-confidence typical of the 'Guides', Gen Lefebvre-Desnoëttes ordered his 600 men to attack, without reconnoitring, or even deploying his squadrons properly.

They were facing about the same number of sabres from the British 10th and 18th Hussars and three troops of the 3rd

Hussars, King's German Legion, but few of these were visible. The piquets of the 18th at first fell back, but when joined by the KGL troopers they soon took the initiative by charging and cutting their way through the first French line. Outnumbered, they withdrew towards Benavente village, where LtGen Henry Paget was lying in wait with his reserve of the 10th Hussars. The Mounted Chasseurs and Mamelukes confidently continued their advance under the eyes of Napoleon himself, who had now arrived on the heights overlooking the Ezla. General Paget picked his moment and led the British 10th Hussars in a charge from their concealed position, with the 18th and 3rd KGL elements in support. Paget drove the French back pell-mell towards the riverbank; some tried to swim for it, but many others, their horses already blown, were forced to turn and fight. In the mêlée that followed more than 50 Chasseurs were killed or wounded (among them, for example, Standard-Bearer Baucheux killed and Capt Geist wounded); and 72 were taken prisoner, including Gen

Lefebvre-Desnoëttes himself. (Credit for his capture was afterwards disputed between Pte Grisdall of the 10th – who would be promoted to sergeant by the Prince Regent in person – and Pte Bergmann of the KGL.) British losses in this skirmish were about 50 killed, wounded and missing.

Two days later, in a letter to the Empress, Napoleon wrote that Lefebvre-Desnoëttes had charged the enemy with 300 Chasseurs, suffering many dead, and that the general, whose horse was wounded, was saved from drowning by the British. He asked Josephine to console his wife. The same day, in another letter to his brother King Joseph, he expressed his grief that his beloved 'Guides' had suffered this serious setback; but he claimed (with his usual dishonesty) that Lefebvre-Desnoëttes had faced 3,000 enemy cavalry! He rewrote this first serious defeat in the regiment's history – which was due solely to Lefebvre-Desnoëttes' impetuosity, and Paget's skill – into an act of heroism; he tried to obtain the general's exchange for a captured British senior officer, and although this proved vain he kept Lefebvre-Desnoëttes on the rolls as colonel of the Mounted Chasseurs.

\* \* \*

News of mobilization in Austria forced Napoleon to leave the pursuit of Gen Moore to Marshal Soult (who caught up with the British at Corunna, but was unable to prevent their embarkation). Returning to France, the Emperor soon recalled his Guard from Spain.

On 11 January 1809 he ordered the Mounted Chasseurs and Polish Light Horse, stationed at Valladolid, to march the next day for Vittoria via Burgos and Miranda. The regimental depots in Madrid were to leave the city for Vittoria, where the regiments were to await further instructions. The next day, Gen Guyot was ordered to place Mounted Chasseur piquets along the roads to France in order to escort the Emperor back to Paris. On 15 January the formal order to withdraw both Guard light cavalry regiments, the Mounted Grenadiers, Dragoons, Foot Chasseurs and Grenadiers from Spain was given in a letter to Marshal Bessières, who was to stay behind for a time as commander-in-chief of the Guard troops serving in Spain. In the end, all Guard regiments were recalled, but – with the exception of the Polish Light Horse – each had to leave one squadron or two companies behind in Spain. Napoleon left Bayonne on 19 January, to arrive unexpectedly only three days later at the gates of his palace in Paris.

The distance the Emperor covered in three days usually took regiments at least three weeks or a month. On 21 January, the Mounted Chasseurs received orders to reunite all their detachments and depot at Tolosa, leaving there for Paris via Bordeaux and Poitiers on the 27th. After the first eight days' marching they were given a day of rest, and thereafter one day's rest for every four days on the march, until the final stage, again of seven days. On 27 February 1809, Gen Guyot left Tolosa with 928 men, 1,000 horses and six wagons from the Mounted Chasseurs, Mamelukes and Light Horse of Berg, who arrived in Bayonne on 1 March and left again soon afterwards. Another detachment left Bayonne on 22 March with 250 men and horses commanded by Maj Corbineau; they were to arrive in Paris on 23 April, but to save three days they were forced to leave the slow artillery units behind them.

When crossing the border from Spain even the army was subjected to detailed formalities by customs officers; but the Guard would not have been the Guard if they had accepted the same treatment as Line regiments. On 5 April 1809 a report from the Ministry of War arrived on the Emperor's desk: the minister had received a complaint from his colleague the Minister of Finance, responsible for Customs. It seemed that on 3 March a convoy of the Mounted Chasseurs, led by SgtMaj Vasceille, had refused to submit to checks at the border. Nor was this an isolated case; a week previously another convoy of the regiment, commanded by a captain, had also run across the border without stopping.

## 1809: Wagram

On the night of 21/22 March 1809, 35 officers and 738 men from the Guard cavalry, Mounted Artillery and Train, commanded by Gen Arrighi, left Paris for Germany. With them were 11 officers and 200 men from the Mounted Chasseurs, who had to be in Metz on 4 April. Six days later an Austrian army under Archduke Charles invaded the territory of France's ally Bavaria, and another under Archduke John was on the march towards Italy via the Julian Alps. The War of the Fifth Coalition had started.

Detail from painting by C.P. Gautherot of Napoleon being wounded at Ratisbonne in 1809. This captain of the Mounted Chasseurs – note triple-chevron sleeve braiding – wears the deerskin breeches of the duty squadron and escort. The scarlet bag of his colback shows three gold pipings, perhaps on the seams and in the centre. Clearly visible is his black leather pouch with gold edging and gilt eagle on the flap.

In late April the regiment was in Strasbourg. Most of their arms, equipment and full dress were packed in large portmanteaux labelled with the troopers' names, and placed in wagons that would follow the regiment. Leaving in groups of 25, they wore their *habits*, colbacks and overalls, and apart from their sabres carried only a portemanteau with some spare linen. Joining up in Germany with their detachments coming from Spain, they arrived on 2 May in Stuttgart, where the following day they were inspected by the King of Württemberg.

The Mounted Chasseurs of the Guard saw no action in the first engagements of the Austrian campaign: Eckmühl (22 April), and the bloody two-day battles of Aspern and Essling (21–22 May). While Lefebvre-Desnoëttes retained his rank in captivity, Maj Guyot received on 5 June the title of *colonel commandant en second*. Major Thiry was promoted general of brigade in the Line, and SqnLdrs Daumesnil and Corbineau became majors on 13 June.

While Napoleon worked on his plans in captured Vienna, on 28 June a report from Marshal Berthier reached him at the Schönbrunn Palace. Joseph Domingue, *dit* 'Hercule', who had served for a decade in the Guides, and was now retired with the reward

*(continued on page 33)*

GUIDES DE BONAPARTE
1: Guide, Italy, 1796–97
2: Guide, Egypt, 1798–99
3: Officer, Egypt, 1798–99

A

GARDE CONSULAIRE
1: Chasseur, full dress, 1803–04
2: Chasseur; uniform for service in attendance on the First Consul, 1803–04
3: Trumpeter; uniform for service in attendance on the First Consul, 1803–04

B

GARDE IMPÉRIALE
1 & 2: Chasseurs, uniform for service in attendance on the Emperor, 1804–15
3: Chasseur, *grande tenue ordinaire*

1

2

3

P. Courcelle

D

E

P. Courcelle

ORDERS OF FULL DRESS
1: Officer, *grande tenue de parade,* 1810–15
2: Officer, *grande tenue ordinaire*, 1805–15
3: Officer, Imperial escort piquet, 1810–15
4: Senior officer, winter full dress, 1804–15

FIELD SERVICE DRESS, 1805-15
1: Chasseur, duty squadron, *tenue de campagne*
2: Chasseur, *tenue de campagne, service ordinaire*
3: Officer, summer field dress, c.1812

P. Courcelle

**G**

MUSICIANS
1: Mounted kettle-drummer, c.1804–05
2: Trumpet-major, *seconde tenue de parade*
3: Trumpeter, duty squadron, parade full dress

of a commission as *chef de bataillon* in the Royal African Battalion, was in deep trouble. The unit's administrative council, of which he was chairman by virtue of his rank, had taken advantage of his inability to read or write and his consequent inability to supervise the battalion's accountancy. As a result of their villainy a deficit of 40,000 francs had been discovered, of which Hercule was liable for repaying 50 per cent out of his own pocket. The Minister of War had ordered that 20 per cent of his pension should be held back until the full amount was paid off. Hercule had already complained about the administrative malpractices in his unit; therefore Berthier asked that – given his age, wounds and fine career – repayment should be foregone. Still looking after the wellbeing of his former Guides, Napoleon agreed, and Hercule was again granted his full pension.

A naïve but well-detailed painting showing Lt Grillon charging, in full dress. This shows clearly that the plume was not fixed to the front of the colback but to the left side. It also shows the officer's panther-skin saddle cover, with the tail flapping loose in front of his leg – the lining is shown as white. (Army Museum, Brussels)

A week later, Napoleon returned to the Danube crossings denied him at Aspern/Essling, to fight another costly two-day battle against Archduke Charles at Wagram (5–6 July 1809). On the evening of 3 July the Mounted Chasseurs received the order to cross from the west bank to the concentration area on the island of Lobau, and on the night of 4/5 July they crossed again to the east bank. On the 5th both armies took up their positions and small-scale combats took place; and at about 4am on the 6th a battle started which would involve some 400,000 men and 800 guns on both sides. The fighting swung first one way and then another; Napoleon ordered a 'grand battery' of 100 guns to blow a hole through the Austrian centre, where Gen Macdonald's division, supported by the Guards cavalry, launched a massed attack towards the village of Süssenbrünn. This finally ground to a halt with heavy loss; but then Davout's III Corps destroyed the Austrian left wing, where Archduke John had failed to come up in support.

The Mounted Chasseurs lost a number of officers and men to artillery fire before they were ordered forward to deal with the Austrian Gen Kollawrath's infantry squares in front of the French left, which resulted in their capturing four guns. When the Austrians finally retreated there were few French troops who were not too exhausted to mount a pursuit, but among them were the Mounted Chasseurs and Polish Light Horse of the Guard, both of which were well mounted and still in good shape. Colonel Guyot was ordered to take both regiments and to *'charger à fond'* – to drive the enemy to the bitter end.

Arriving on a hillside overlooking the Vienna-Brno road, Guyot saw large columns of Austrian cavalry and infantry retreating in good order. Without losing a moment he ordered a charge on the cavalry, which consisted of two dragoon and two lancer regiments. These were all driven off, leaving four infantry regiments apparently at the mercy of the Chasseurs and Poles. Guyot ordered the first two squadrons of the Mounted Chasseurs to attack them; but they had already formed three massive squares, and the Chasseurs were received with heavy volleys. Seeing them hesitate and withdraw, Guyot ordered the rest of his brigade to attempt the task; in the end they just managed to break through one square, while

**33**

the rest of the Austrians withdrew. Casualties for the regiment's brief but fierce engagement at Wagram were heavy; 25 rankers were killed and 123 wounded, and both Maj Corbineau and Maj Daumesnil lost a leg.

After Wagram, on 9 August, Col Guyot was promoted *général de brigade,* and Col Lion from the 14th Mounted Chasseurs of the Line became the third major in the regiment. Late in 1809 the Guard returned to Paris, where the Vélites were once more organized into one squadron of two companies.

# THE INTERBELLUM, 1810–12

While the rest of mainland Europe was now at peace under Napoleon's yoke, in Spain the war rumbled on. After a year's rest, the regiment began to provide squadrons for service there on a rotating basis. One report of 1810 lists among the Guard cavalry in Spain, commanded by Gen Lepic, 24 officers and 365 men from the Mounted Chasseurs; the same report bears a hastily scribbled note that 120 inexperienced Vélites were serving with the regiment.

From 1 July 1811 no more Vélites were accepted into the Mounted Chasseurs, Mounted Grenadiers, Dragoons or Artillery of the Guard. All those who were already serving would keep their positions as long as they paid their allowances, but newcomers were to be diverted to the Dutch Lancers of the Guard. On 20 July, Marshal Mortier reported to Napoleon that the Mounted Chasseurs had 129 Vélites who had not served at Wagram, of whom 23 were serving in Spain. Another report of the same date listed the strength of the Chasseurs and Mamelukes serving in Spain as 2 squadron-leaders (one of them Mameluke), 3 captains, 15 lieutenants, and 293 NCOs, Chasseurs, Vélites and Mamelukes. The official disbanding of the Vélites on 1 August coincided with the formation of a 5th Squadron in the Mounted Chasseurs; on 6 August there were still 131 Vélites with the regiment. The next day a report indicated that the regiment still had 104 of all ranks who had been Guides in Italy and Egypt.

Further changes were decreed on 16 December 1811, when Gen Guyot was promoted to the army rank of *général de division* while retaining his command of the regiment. New senior officers had arrived during previous months: Col d'Haurangeville, a relative of Marshal Berthier (6 August), and Gen Excelmans (24 December), were commissioned as regimental majors to replace Majs Corbineau and Daumesnil.

With the exception of the regimental detachments serving in Spain, the Chasseurs' main functions during 1810 and 1811 were to escort the Emperor or the Imperial couple on their travels around the empire and to all the many ceremonies that took place. To show the extent of such escorts: during their state visit to the newly annexed territories of Holland, 1,302 Guard cavalrymen escorted

Jean-Baptiste Gutschenreiter (1782–1859) served in the Light Horse Regiment of the Grand Duchy of Berg before transferring into the Mounted Chasseurs on 11 January 1807. A sergeant-major in 1809 and sub-lieutenant in 1811, he became a full lieutenant on 27 February 1813. He was admitted to the Legion of Honour that April, and was wounded at Hanau in October, being appointed a *sous adjudant-major* in December. After Napoleon's first abdication he entered the Corps Royal des Chevau-légers de France, which would become the Lancers of the Imperial Guard during the Hundred Days. Lieutenant Gutschenreiter is portrayed here in 1818, wearing a later style of the pelisse recognizable by its short waist. Next to his cross of the Legion of Honour he dislays the blue-ribboned Order of the Lily that he received during the First Restoration. (Private collection, France)

them (347 Polish Lancers, 276 Dutch Lancers, 335 Mounted Chasseurs, 140 Dragoons, 137 Mounted Grenadiers and 67 Gendarmes d'élite). An interesting report shows the surprisingly high number of Mounted Chasseurs who entered hospital between 1 January 1810 and 1 January 1811:

| | |
|---|---|
| In hospital on 1 January 1810: | 122 |
| Entering hospital between those dates: | 429 |
| Leaving hospital between those dates: | 504 |
| Died in hospital: | 19 |
| In hospital on 1 January 1811: | 28 |

\* \* \*

After two years of relative peace, in late 1811 the political situation deteriorated; instead of troops marching south towards the Peninsula, they would now begin to move east. All Guard units were recalled from Spain, the first detachments leaving for France in mid-December 1811. A detachment arriving in Paris on 30 January 1812 – consisting of 24 officers, 551 NCOs and troopers with 234 horses – included an officer, 67 troopers and 10 horses of the Mounted Chasseurs. On 18 December 1811 the regiment numbered:

| *Mounted Chasseurs* | | *Mamelukes* | |
|---|---|---|---|
| Present: | 828 | Present: | 43 |
| Absent: | 97 | Absent: | 1 |
| In hospital: | 69 | In hospital: | – |
| On leave: | – | On leave: | – |
| Serving in Spain: | 287 | Serving in Spain: | 72 |
| Prisoners of war: | 27 | Prisoners of war: | 27 |
| *Total:* | *1,308* | *Total:* | *116* |
| Establishment: | 1,372 | Establishment: | 160 |
| Shortfall: | 64 | Shortfall: | 44 |

On 23 January 1812 the regiment was 118 horses short of establishment, and a Guard detachment, taking saddles and harness with them, left Compiègne for Hanover to collect remounts.

A week later, at Napoleon's request, Grand Marshal Duroc reported on the staff officers of the cavalry of the Guard. For the Mounted Chasseurs he indicated that Gen Guyot commanded the regiment and that they had at present four majors: Lion, d'Haugerauville, Excelmans – and still, surprisingly, Daumesnil. This was one major too many, and Duroc proposed to promote the one-legged Daumesnil to general of brigade and appoint him governor of the fortress of Vincennes.

# THE LATER CAMPAIGNS

### 1812: Russia

On 29 February 1812, Napoleon instructed Bessières that the Mounted Chasseurs, Mounted Grenadiers and Dragoons should leave Paris in three columns on 2, 3 and 4 March. He only wanted some 1,000 men of his Guard cavalry to stay in the capital. One of the detachments was commanded by Maj Lion; the Mounted Chasseurs in it were commanded by Maj d'Haugerauville, and consisted of SqnLdr Joannes,

1 captain adjutant-major, 1 lieutenant sub adjutant-major, 2 surgeons, 3 captains, 5 first lieutenants and 4 second lieutenants, 4 officiers of the *petit état-major*, and 320 Chasseurs.

On 26 March a new detachment of 670 Guardsmen, including 100 Mounted Chasseurs, also headed east; this was followed on 15 April by another, destined for Mainz and numbering 1,030, of whom 300 were Mounted Chasseurs. The remaining elements of Guard cavalry were to leave their barracks on 18 April, leaving only 150 experienced Chasseurs and Gen Guyot in Paris to escort the Emperor, whom they would follow to Dresden and the Polish-Russian border. In fact the speed and distances involved were so extreme that even Guyot had to abandon the Emperor on occasion.

On 6 May, Gen Lefebvre-Desnoëttes returned from captivity in Britain after successfully escaping (many said, by breaking his oath of parole). Once he was back, even though Gen Guyot had been leading the regiment since he had got himself captured in Spain, Lefebvre-Desnoëttes resumed command.

There is no space here for another repetition of more than the broad outlines of the Russian campaign. After crossing the River Niemen with their Emperor the Imperial Guard would see little or no action during the advancing phase. Always pulled deeper and deeper into the vast steppes by the retreating Russians, and suffering serious losses – especially of horses – from exhaustion, the torrid weather and the shortage of food and water, the Grande Armée arrived in burning Moscow on 15 September 1812. With lines of communication so stretched, the storehouses emptying, the winter season advancing and all hopes for an honourable peace abandoned, the French army left the half-ruined city on 19 October; the Imperial Guard had already left, marching southwards from their quarters near the Kaluga Gate, on the 14th.

On 24 October, Prince Eugène's IV Corps, serving as vanguard, encountered the Russians at Malojaroslawetz. That night the Emperor stayed in the small village of Gorodnya, and next day he left his tented 'palace' at daybreak to visit the battlefield. A Polish Guard Lancers platoon commanded by Lt Hempel opened the road, followed by Napoleon, his escort piquet of Mounted Chasseurs and his immediate staff; behind them rode the 200-strong duty squadron of Mounted Chasseurs commanded by SqnLdr Kirmann; and finally, at some distance, the other three duty squadrons (one from each Old Guard cavalry regiment).

With little warning the column was attacked by a pack of 3,000 to 4,000 Cossacks. Kirmann and his duty squadron, supported by Napoleon's ADCs and staff officers, charged the advancing enemy at odds of one against 20, and were soon forced to retreat. Unaware of Napoleon's presence, however, and merely looking for booty, the Cossacks turned to looting a nearby artillery park. Marshal Bessières had meanwhile rallied the other duty squadrons, which he led against the marauders, inflicting severe casualties and forcing them to flee empty-handed. The Mounted Chasseurs lost 9 men killed and 7 wounded, the latter including SqnLdr Kirmann and Capt Schmidt.

What had been intended as an offensive campaign south of Moscow soon became a full retreat towards the Niemen. The Mounted Chasseurs of the Guard still protected the Emperor and, when

Napoleon abandoned his snowbound army on 5 December to return to Paris, they organized an escort to see him safely on his way. When they finally crossed back over the Niemen into Poland only a minority of the survivors were still mounted; the regiment retreated as best it could across Poland and Germany via Posen and Berlin.

## 1813: Rebuilding the regiment

To restore the regiment's strength, Gen Lefebvre-Desnoëttes returned to France with two dozen officers and NCOs, while all the dismounted survivors were concentrated near the Vistula river. Meanwhile, Gen Guyot and those who were still mounted and capable of service with the army played their part in trying to hold off the advancing Sixth Coalition allies. On 5 January 1813, based on the roll calls for the squadrons in the field on 3 December 1812, the Mounted Chasseurs (including depots and those serving in France) numbered:

95 officers (of which 13 Mamelukes); 1,569 rankers (of which 90 Mamelukes, and not including 25 *élèves-trompettes* serving in the regiment); and 959 horses (of which 45 from the Mamelukes). In all the Mamelukes were short of 57 men and 42 horses; the Mounted Chasseurs needed 561 horses, but in fact exceeded the normal regimental field strength by 1 officer and 208 rankers.

A better view of the state of the Guard cavalry may be gained from a report written by Duroc in January 1813; in this he stated that the available personnel could be divided into three categories:

(1) Those who were mounted and still able to serve with the army near the Vistula, consisting of 1,000–1,100 men with horses.

(2) Those who were arriving at the Vistula unmounted; these consisted of some 1,100 soldiers (200 Dutch Lancers, 300 Mounted Chasseurs, 300 Dragoons and 300 Mounted Grenadiers). These could be sent to Mainz to find the necessary mounts and equipment.

(3) Those who were in France and fit to serve – for the moment, the only reserve of Guard cavalry. Each cavalry regiment, except the Polish Lancers of the Guard, had a number of officers and men from whom Duroc hoped to organize eight squadrons, two from each regiment, to total 2,100 mounted men. To reach this number he still needed 70 officers, 1,342 troopers and 1,515 horses. The Mounted Chasseurs had 4 officers, 250 troopers and 180 horses in Paris. To organize the two squadrons for the army, Duroc needed 19 officers, 250 men and 320 horses, which had to come from units serving in Spain, with horses to be provided by the Confederation of the Rhine.

During the hideous retreat of the dying Grande Armée across Russia nearly all Line regiments had lost not only most of their strength but also

On campaign, two of Napoleon's immediate entourage were the *Chasseurs de portefeuille*, who carried large leather satchels containing maps of the immediate area. This detail from a painting by Vernet shows the portfolio, as well as the double shoulder belt supporting both the pouch and the carbine. The saddle portemanteau shows a bugle-horn Chasseur emblem on the end, but this may be a mistaken interpretation by an artist working well after the period.

Men of the Young Guard squadrons of the regiment (6th–9th Sqns) formed in 1813. These were sent to Belgium to serve with the army intended to protect the northern part of France from Allied invasion in 1814; under the overall command of Gen Maison, they served in the region Antwerp-Brussels-Lille. They are reconstructed here in full dress, showing the scarlet *shako rouleau* with yellow trim and cap cords, dark green dolman with scarlet cuffs, scarlet pelisse (not, in fact, a regulation item for these squadrons), scarlet breeches, and yellow/gold 'metal'. (Army Museum, Brussels)

their morale, and more than one had simply disappeared. The only units still more or less viable as fighting corps were the regiments of the Guard. Knowing that his new army would have to be scraped together mainly from newly levied conscripts, Napoleon therefore reorganized his Guard on a much larger scale than ever before.[5]

### Old and Young Guard

On 18 January 1813, at the Tuileries Palace, Napoleon signed a new decree that would raise the number of squadrons in the regiment to eight; with 250 men in each, the Mounted Chasseurs should muster 2,000 men. On 6 March he raised the figure again, to nine squadrons plus the Mamelukes as 10th Sqn, giving a regimental establishment of 2,500 men.

All the soldiers then serving in the regiment, and those who would now enter it with the required qualifications, would be considered and paid as Old Guard, and would be known (and addressed) as '1st Chasseurs'. The men gathered in by conscription, or 'offered' by the regional departments, would be known and addressed as '2nd Chasseurs'; these would receive the pay of Line units, plus a supplement granted to troops serving in Paris. The Old Guard would provide the 1st to 5th Squadrons, and the Young Guard the 6th to 9th. These junior, Young Guard squadrons would wear visibly different uniforms.

Loyalty to the Emperor and regimental ésprit de corps among the Mounted Chasseurs' Old Guard personnel had survived the recent disastrous campaign. One-third of the Old Guard troopers were veterans of Russia, and the rest were selected from cavalry regiments serving in Spain. Despite an increased number of companies the senior command hardly changed at all. General Lefebvre-Desnoëttes was still the *colonel en premier* while Gen Guyot served as *colonel en second*. The *majors* (note, again, that this was a regimental appointment, not a rank) were ColMaj Lion, commanding the Old Guard, and ColMaj Meuziau commanding the Young Guard squadrons. Nearly all the troopers wore the cross of the Legion of Honour or the Italian Order of the Iron Crown, which brought annual bonuses of 600–800 francs.

Early in 1813, Marshal Bessières, commander-in-chief of the Guard cavalry, organized the departure of detachments for the army in the field. The Chasseurs, like the other cavalry units, were divided into two *régiments de marche*; and as the 1st Regt de Marche comprised only 400 men, Bessières requested authorization to add the 1st Sqn of the 2nd Regt de Marche to it. His reason was the more intensive nature of the Mounted Chasseurs' duties when with the Emperor in the field, and he stated that they would always need one-fifth more men than the other Guard cavalry regiments.

---

5 Even the Guard was not without its disappointments in Russia, however; several officers of the Dragoons were expelled from the regiment for leaving the ranks, sometimes to plunder regimental wagons. Early in 1813, in Paris alone, there were some 500 Guardsmen in prison for desertion.

One by one, combined detachments from the Guard cavalry regiments left Paris for Germany; for example, one on 5 March 1813, with 968 men and 1,068 horses, of whom 125 were Mounted Chasseurs with an equal number of horses, and some 68 were former Gendarmes d'Espagne who, once they arrived with the army, were to be divided between the Mounted Chasseurs, Mounted Grenadiers and Dragoons. On 10 April another detachment left Paris, crossing the Rhine at Strasbourg on 1 May and arriving in Dresden nine days later. One of the officers in this detachment was 2nd Lt Parquin, who served in the 10th Co commanded by Capt Klein de Kleinenberg, brother-in-law of ColMaj Lion; the 10th and 5th Cos would form the 5th Squadron.

On 16 April, Gen Guyot left Paris for Mainz, where he arrived four days later; there he was instructed by Napoleon to follow him as commander of his escort, which would consist of 450 troopers of the Guard cavalry.

## The German campaign

The start of the 1813 campaign seemed to be successful, with victories such as Lützen and Bautzen; but these were in fact only half-victories, since the lack of French cavalry prevented the pursuit of the beaten Coalition armies. Before the armistice of Pleswitz, signed on 5 June 1813, the Mounted Chasseurs of the Guard did not participate in any engagements; this would change after hostilities resumed on 16 August.

At Dresden on 27 August, without seeing much action, the regiment suffered from enemy fire as it sat under continuous heavy rain. The regimental paymaster, 2nd Lt Brice, had his horse shot from under him. This brought him to the notice of Gen Lefebvre-Desnoëttes, who severely reprimanded him for being on the battlefield – he was more useful in Dresden, with the regimental funds and his account books.

The Emperor found that when he manoeuvred personally against one of the Coalition armies it retreated and refused battle, while another attacked one of the detached French corps (advice supposedly given to the Tsar by the exiled French general Moreau, who was mortally wounded at Dresden). These tactics forced Napoleon to march from one place to another without pinning and defeating his opponents, while his detached forces were beaten and pushed back one by one.

## Leipzig

In the autumn the Coalition armies finally closed in on Napoleon for the huge three-day battle around Leipzig. On the first day, 16 October 1813, the regiment was placed behind Gen Drouot's 100-gun Guard battery. It was only at dusk that Gen Letort, commander of the Dragoons of the Guard, was ordered to take one squadron from each regiment – a force of 1,000 sabres – to support Marshal Oudinot's corps in the path of Gen Schwartzenberg's advancing army. Threatened by the Austrian cavalry, the French infantry had already formed squares when Letort's cavalry passed between them, and formed for battle in front of them just as the enemy were on the brink of a charge. The Guard cavalry kicked forward to meet the charge on the move, overrunning the Austrians and putting them to flight. The enemy right-wing unit – the Latour Dragoons – were not involved and continued forward, getting themselves cut off from the rest of the Austrian cavalry and becoming easy prey for the Mounted

Chasseurs and Dragoons squadrons, who cut them down and took 200 prisoners.

On the second day of the battle the regiment was not involved. On the afternoon of 18 October, Napoleon's former allies – the Saxon corps and Württemberg cavalry – suddenly changed sides, leaving an enormous gap in the French lines. Informed about the defection, Napoleon ordered Gen Nansouty to follow him with the entire cavalry of the Guard. The Russians and Swedes were already marching en masse for the gap, confident of meeting no resistance. The shock effect of being hit by five crack Guard cavalry regiments – about 8,000 of probably the best-trained cavalry on the field – was considerable. The infantry columns were thrown back in disorder, and the Russian Gen Bennigsen was nearly captured. However, the Guard cavalry then came under heavy canister- and grape-shot fire from the strong Russian artillery, and were forced to retreat.

At Leipzig, Lt Parquin of the 10th Co witnessed an example of soldierly devotion to the Emperor when one of his rankers had his horse shot from under him. Normally this meant that the man would have eight to ten days to go and collect himself a remount from the Guard depot, so Parquin was surprised to notice him back in the ranks before the end of the battle. Asked how he had managed to find a remount so quickly, the soldier replied that since he had been awarded annual bonuses in recognition of past service, he always kept one year's cash sewn inside his belt in case he needed to spend it in order to continue his service near the Emperor.

At nightfall on 18 October, outnumbered and with ammunition running low, the army was ordered to retreat. During that last day the Mounted Chasseurs suffered 14 killed, and among the wounded was Capt Oudinot, eldest son of Marshal Nicolas-Charles Oudinot.

**Born in Paris on 20 December 1786,** Denis-Charles Parquin entered the army at the age of 16 and progressed through the ranks of corporal, quartermaster, sergeant and sub-lieutenant with the Grande Armée from 1805 until 1807, when he was wounded at Eylau. He returned to serve in Austria in 1809 and in Spain until 1813, when he was commissioned second lieutenant in the Mounted Chasseurs. In this 19th-century lithograph Parquin is represented as an officer of the Old Guard in full dress.

### Hanau

Nothing could stop the Coalition armies, and Napoleon retreated right across Germany towards the French border. Once again, on more than one occasion the Mounted Chasseurs had to face about to discourage hovering Russian Cossacks.

After the defeat at Leipzig the French-allied German states of the Confederation of the Rhine changed sides one by one; and at Hanau on 20 October the French vanguard ran into elements of some 60,000 Bavarian troops under Gen Wrede, seeking to cut off their retreat in the face of the other Coalition armies. Before arriving at the gates of the town the French had to cross the forest of Lamboy, infested with Bavarian snipers, and once out of it they were faced by a 58-gun battery (though in fact Wrede had failed to bring up adequate ammunition). Napoleon, aware that he could not wait for the rest of his embattled army to join him, tried to break through the Bavarians with a few units, supported by the 50-gun Guard artillery under command of Gen Drouot. Wrede – whose dispositions did him no credit as a veteran of Napoleon's campaigns – ordered his cavalry to take the French artillery; and just at that moment Gen Nansouty arrived with the Guard cavalry.

In a few minutes they overran and dispersed four enemy cavalry regiments; then they turned on the surprised Bavarian infantry before they had time to form squares. Captain Schmidt, at the head of a squadron of Mounted Chasseurs, forced two infantry battalions to surrender near the gates of Hanau. With his left flank beaten back into the River Kinzig, Gen Wrede was forced to retreat, leaving behind some 6,500 casualties, and the road open for the French to continue their retreat and cross the Rhine at Mainz. Casualties were light among the Mounted Chasseurs: just 4 killed and a dozen wounded. Among the latter was Lt Parquin, who took a bayonet stab in the face; his behaviour at Hanau saw him promoted to captain in the regiment's Young Guard. Captain Oudinot, aged 20, distinguished himself at the head of his squadron by retaking a battery of six guns lost by the Guard artillery, and capturing the entire Bavarian infantry battalion that had taken them. As a token of gratitude the Emperor took off his own Legion of Honour decoration and awarded it to the already decorated Oudinot, raising him to the class of Officer in the Legion.

## 1814: The campaign of France

At the end of 1813 the Emperor, once more obliged to re-create his army after losses numbered in the hundreds of thousands, called for all retired soldiers of the Guard to report for duty. The reaction was such that the local prefects, the Minister of War and even the ADCs of the Emperor were overwhelmed with letters from former guardsmen offering their services. Some of them were invalids, having lost a leg. One retired officer who volunteered, the former trumpeter and lieutenant Krettly, was in fact to serve in the National Guard.

## Officers' Roll, Mounted Chasseurs of the Imperial Guard

The names are as they appear in the 1813 *Almanach Impérial*.
Decorations are indicated thus:
*Legion of Honour* * = Knight; O* = Officer; C* = Commander.
*Imperial Order of the Reunion* GC# = Grand Cross.

### Regimental Staff
Colonel: GenDiv Count Lefebvre-Desnoëttes (C*, GC#)
2nd Colonel: GenDiv Baron Guyot (C*)
Major: Col Baron Lion (O*)
Major: vacant (Col Baron Meuziau was commissioned LtCol in
  the regiment 14 May 1813)

Chevalier Joannes (O*) – Squadron Leader; Rabusson (O*) – SqnLdr;
Chevalier Bayeux (O*) – SqnLdr; Labiffe (O*) – SqnLdr;
Lafite (O*) – SqnLdr; Vanot (*) – SqnLdr; Debelle – SqnLdr;
Trobriant – SqnLdr; Guiot (*) – Quartermaster; Bellebaux (O*) – QM;
Cayre (*) – QM; Spitzer – Captain Instructor;
Sève (*) – Capt Adjutant Major; Assant (*) – Capt AdjMaj;
Keraval (*) – 1st Lt Sub-AdjMaj;, Vazillier (*) – 1st Lt Sub-AdjMaj;
Boizeau – 1st Lt Sub-AdjMaj; Frot – 2nd Lt Sub-AdjMaj;
Spigre (*) – 2nd Lt Sub-AdjMaj; Lecoq (*) – 2nd Lt Sub-AdjMaj;
L'Hernault – 2nd Lt Sub-AdjMaj; Lequatre – 2nd Lt Sub-AdjMaj;
Dackweiller – 2nd Lt Sub-AdjMaj; Maziau (*) – Capt Admin Adj;
Danchery (*) – 1st Lt Admin Adj; Perrier (O*) – 1st Lt Standard-Bearer;
Bayard (*) – 1st Lt SB; Allié (*) – 2nd Lt SB; Billard (*) – 2nd Lt SB;

Lachaume (*) – Surgeon Major; Ferrus (*) – SM;
Pergot (*) – Assistant SM; Faure – Asst SM; Demerlot – Asst SM;
vacant – Asst SM; vacant – Asst SM

### Captains
Parizot (O*), Le Brasseur (*), Schmidt (*), Moysant (*), Bro (*),
Deville (*), Achintre (*), Blanquefort (*), Gay (*), Comte Oudinot (*),
Barbanègre (O*), de Kleinenberg (*), Decoux, Rocourt, Lemercier,
Larivière, Bellancourt, Pierre

### 1st Lieutenants
Lambert (O*), Dupont (*), Viala (*), Cabart (*), Darmagnac (*), Bugat (*),
Décalogne (*), Rudelle (*), Gutschenreiter, Allimant (*), Mey de Chales
(*), Moutard (*), Enjubeault (*), Brice (*), Helson (*), Durand (*), Rolin (*),
d'Equevilly, Laclos, Lespinasse, Goudmetz (*), Leroy, Sanglier, Girard
*dit* Vieux, Nolette, Stéphanopoli, Limbourg, L'Etang, Toulongeon,
Blot, Foulon, Bonnet (*), Delor (*), Jomini, Jouglas, Sabatier, Ziekel

### 2nd Lieutenants
Forcioli (*), Blandin (*), Chapelle (*), Gaillet (*), Oswald (*), Pescheur (*),
Beller, Jallot, Rouxelin de Formigny, Vanheulle, Brice, Marcheret,
Mertens, François, Poirot de Valcourt, Fisher, Lapôtre, Henneson (*),
Benard (*), Mathey (*), Velay, Pigault-Lebrun, Crucq, Robin (*), Buchot,
Delentivi (*), Vieil, Parquin (*), Lagouz-Duplessis (*), Salmon,
Bailleul (*), Lagaune (*), Demange, Chiret, Favre, Miret

On 1 December 1813, Gen Guyot received the command of the Mounted Grenadiers of the Guard, leaving the regiment without a *colonel en second*.

Judging that the Coalition would invade France via the Low Countries, Napoleon concentrated a large part of his Guard in Belgium (his staff even considered moving all Guard depots to Lille). The Mounted Chasseurs were split in two: 1st–5th Sqns, plus 11th Co from 6th Sqn, all commanded by Gen Lion (who had been promoted *général de brigade* on 23 June 1813), stayed with the Emperor, while the Young Guard squadrons, commanded by ColMaj Meuziau, went with Gen Lefebvre-Desnoëttes to Belgium. But the situation suddenly changed when the Coalition armies chose to move into France by the more southerly routes, crossing the Swiss border and the Rhine in Germany.

On 3 January 1814 the Mounted Chasseurs had already left Paris for Reims when Gen Lefebvre-Desnoëttes was recalled from Belgium, leaving the Young Guard squadrons in the hands of Gen Castex. In the past, with the exception of the second half of the 1813 German campaign, the Guard cavalry had been kept in reserve, and only committed in order to save critical situations such as those at Austerlitz and Eylau. Now, however, they would have to support the less experienced Line cavalry regiments as a matter of routine.

In the bitter conditions of early 1814, the always outnumbered Mounted Chasseurs served with honour in many engagements against the Coalition armies. One of their acts of bravery was noted on 28 February, when Lt Allimant took 17 rankers out on a reconnaissance. This was a campaign in which river crossings played a crucial part; and at La Ferté-Gaucher, Allimant sighted an enemy pontoon train escorted by a squadron of cavalry. In the old Guides tradition that nothing was too big to attack, Allimant's little troop threw themselves on the enemy with shouts of *'Vive l'Empereur!'* and drove them off, bringing 13 pontoons, a forge, two caissons, 98 horses and 64 prisoners back to their general.

But neither audacity, nor the Emperor's undiminished tactical genius, were enough to defeat the enemy armies converging on the capital. Paris capitulated; Napoleon was forced to surrender unconditionally on 11 April 1814; and shortly thereafter he exchanged his empire for a mini-state on the Mediterranean island of Elba.

## The First Restoration

By royal ordinance of the restored King Louis XVIII on 12 May 1814, the Young Guard squadrons of the

OPPOSITE **On campaign Napoleon preferred to wear this undress uniform of the Mounted Chasseurs of the Guard with the epaulettes of colonel; for parades or great occasions he would choose the full dress of the Foot Grenadiers, thus honouring both his senior household regiments. He would be buried in the Mounted Chasseurs uniform. (Collection du Musée National du Château de Malmaison)**

Mounted Chasseurs were disbanded, while the Old Guard element – still commanded by Gen Lefebvre-Desnoëttes and ColMaj Lion – adopted the new title of Corps Royal des Chasseurs de France. They mustered 100 officers and 1,363 NCOs and troopers, but were soon reduced to a peacetime establishment of 55 officers and 644 rankers. They had to leave their Paris barracks and their premier role as the Imperial bodyguard, for the small town of Saumur near the River Loire. All benefits they had received during years of service were reduced by 50 per cent, such as the pension linked to the Legion of Honour. Those who had to leave the army – *les demi-soldes* – were thrown into penury.

On 1 January 1815 the regiment were ordered to leave their barracks at Saumur for those at Cambrai. They were nearly settled in when they heard the momentous news of Napoleon's escape from Elba on 28 February, of his return to French soil and his march towards Paris, gathering men as he went.

### 1815: The Hundred Days

While most commanders waited to see how things developed before committing themselves, Gen Lefebvre-Desnoëttes – in his usual style – placed himself at the head of his regiment and left Cambrai on 9 March for La Fère. His officers were unaware of his intention to try to win the artillery garrison there over to Napoleon's cause. Lefebvre-Desnoëttes marched from one garrison to another, sometimes gaining support, sometimes the opposite. Even within his own ranks some refused to follow him further, including Gen Lion. Seeing that it was impossible to convince his officers, Lefebvre-Desnoëttes left with a handful of men to look for the Emperor, ordering Gen Lion to take the regiment back to Cambrai. It would only be on 20 March that Lefebvre-Desnoëttes joined the Emperor – the day that Napoleon re-entered the Tuileries Palace.

The next day Lefebvre-Desnoëttes saw the command of the Mounted Chasseurs of the Imperial Guard returned to him. With the Guard reconstituted, many former guardsmen returned to their regiments; the Mounted Chasseurs alone received 412 of these. On 15 May, Napoleon decreed the organization of a Mounted Chasseurs regiment of the Young Guard, to be known as the 2nd Mounted Chasseurs and commanded by Gen Merlin de Douai.

Across Europe, Napoleon's return united the other powers into one gigantic coalition. Russia, Britain, the Netherlands, Austria, Italy, Prussia and many other German states all undertook to send their armies marching towards the French borders – though not all of them showed much urgency. Aware that France would be invaded once all these Allied armies had finally gathered into a noose around his frontiers, Napoleon knew that his only chance lay in seizing the initiative. He planned to strike northwards into what is now Belgium, and to engage both of the two most threatening Allied armies – Blücher's Prussians, to the north-east, and Wellington's Anglo-Netherlands-German army, to the north-west – before they could link up; and to this end he crossed the frontier on 15 June.

As usual, the Mounted Chasseurs provided piquets and a duty squadron to escort the Emperor. Once across the border the Mounted Chasseurs, together with the Lancers of the Guard, were detached to support Marshal Ney's effort on 16/17 June to push Wellington's force at Quatre-Bras away from the Prussians, who were retreating from their defeat at Ligny. Not present at Ligny, and seeing practically no action at Quatre-Bras, the Guard light cavalry arrived untouched on the field of Waterloo on the soaking wet night of the 17th.

On 18 June 1815 the Mounted Chasseurs, together with the Lancers of the Guard and commanded by Gen Lefebvre-Desnoëttes, stood in reserve on the east side of the Charleroi road, behind the corps of Gen Drouet d'Erlon and the cuirassiers of Gen Milhaud. The history of the battle of Waterloo, endlessly studied, has thrown up many enigmas. One of them concerns the moment when the cavalry of the Guard got involved in the charges against the centre of Wellington's infantry line, and by what authority, since they could receive direct orders only from the Emperor himself. It is more than probable that, witnessing Marshal Ney's gigantic cavalry charges against the British squares repeatedly failing to break through, they were simply sucked into the battle. They were known for their élan and their vanity in their courage; it is easy to believe that Michel Ney, knowing what hung on the result of this battle, appealed to Lefebvre-Desnoëttes to join his attacks, and that the headstrong general was glad to order his squadrons to advance.

The Mounted Chasseurs were directed towards the 1st Brigade of the King's German Legion, at least part of which had been deployed in line or skirmishing order. When cavalry appeared on their right flank the deployed troops hastily attempted to close up to receive them, as the Lüneburg Light Bn came up in close column to support them. The Chasseurs charged, throwing the Germans into confusion and inflicting significant casualties; among the 74 men of the four KGL battalions killed that day was Col du Plat, the brigade commander, cut down by a Mounted Chasseur, and Capt Klein de Kleinenberg captured one of the battalions' Kings Colour (though he lost it during the retreat).[6]

In the end, the failure of the final attack on Wellington's line, coupled with the steady advance of Blücher's Prussians against the French right flank, forced the Army of the North to retreat in disorder. The Mounted Chasseurs suffered 5 officers and 36 rankers killed at Waterloo, and a high number of wounded and prisoners of war. In the days that followed the regiment, together with the other remnants of the Guard and the army, were sent to the Loire, where they awaited new orders. The 2nd Mounted Chasseurs of the Guard were disbanded between 8 October and 8 November, and the Old Guard element between 26 October and 6 November. By the latter date the old Guides had finally ceased to exist; of the remaining 60 officers and 716 rankers, only two officers and six troopers accepted service in the Royal army. The rest, with a few exceptions, were dismissed or retired.

Veteran NCO – note the service chevrons high on his left sleeve – in late Empire campaign dress. These and the sergeant's chevron above his cuff are in gold; the braiding of his green dolman, the seamstripes of his green breeches and the trim around his collar and cuffs are in mixed scarlet-and-gold. (Drawing by Maurice Toussaint from Marcel Dupont's *Guides de Bonaparte*)

6  The 1st Bde KGL (1st-4th Line Bns) lost 74 killed, 346 wounded and 69 missing on 18 June, from a morning state of 1,910 all ranks.

# PLATE COMMENTARIES

## A1: Guide de Bonaparte, Italy, 1796–97
The colours of what would later become the Imperial livery – dark green, scarlet, and *aurore* – are already evident in the *habit*, vest, and aiguillettes and shoulder knot worn by Bonaparte's mounted bodyguard during the first Italian campaign. The buttons were brass (in French, *cuivre* – copper). The aiguillettes – like the buff hide breeches – were a mark of distinction within the army at that time. Note the short boots, typical of the cavalry of the Revolutionary armies.

## A2: Guide de Bonaparte, Egypt, 1798–99
A native burnous was commonly acquired in place of the cloak. The campaign overalls have black leather booting round the bottom and up the inside leg, and a red stripe edging the side closure, with its many brass buttons. Note the hairstyle, with long braids from the temples and a rear *queue*. The cavalry of the French expeditionary corps disembarked in Egypt with neither mounts nor harness, but Arab horses and saddlery were quickly procured.

## A3: Officer, Guides de Bonaparte, Egypt, 1798–99
This figure, from a contemporary sketch, shows the rear of the *habit* coat, with its red piping and bugle-horn turnback ornaments – here in gold for an officer, like the aiguillettes and the epaulette. Many French cavalry officers in Egypt adopted oriental sabretaches slung from shoulder cords, like the example illustrated. Again, note the Arab saddle and horse furniture; and the sun kerchief worn under the bicorn.

## B1: Chasseur, Consular Guard; full dress, 1803–04
The silhouette is typical for the period, notably the fur colback of modest dimensions. The regimental *grande tenue* is in hussar style. The colback has a scarlet bag or *flamme* piped and tasselled *aurore*, and brass chin-scales; it is dressed with a tall red-over-green plume, and *aurore* cords and flounders. The dark green dolman has a green collar, scarlet cuffs, brass half-ball buttons in rows of 18, and edging and braiding of *aurore* tape and cords; a green and scarlet barrel-sash is worn over it. The scarlet breeches have embroidered thigh knots and sidestripes in *aurore*, and the boots are edged and tasselled in the same shade. The scarlet pelisse, slung from an *aurore* toggle-cord, is trimmed with black fur and has the same buttons, lace and cord braiding as the dolman (it was lined with white flannel). This figure and B2 illustrate the brass-furnished white leather pouch, carbine and waist belts, and the sabre and sabretache; the pouch and sabretache bear Consular motifs incorporating the bugle-horn and the Roman *fasces*. From September 1803 a special Guard pattern light cavalry sabre was issued, with a brass-covered black leather scabbard; in the same year the 1786 pattern hussar musketoon became the issue carbine.

**For the evenings, the Mounted Chasseurs on escort duty were allowed to change into their campaign overalls and to replace the saddle cover with a sheepskin with scarlet edging. The plain scarlet waistcoat with a double row of buttons – *gilet rond* – dates this uniform to before 1804–05. Note the busby plume wrapped in oilcloth to protect it from bad weather. (Drawing by Détaille; Army Museum, Brussels)**

## B2: Chasseur, Consular Guard; uniform for service in attendance on the First Consul, 1803–04
In 1803, *Chef de brigade* Eugène de Beauharnais, who commanded the regiment, issued regulations for the orders of dress which the Chasseurs were to wear on all occasions. This document, which remained in force until the end of the Empire, has come down to us under the title *Cahiers de la Malmaison*. Among other things, it specified that the buff deerskin breeches were to be worn exclusively by those personnel serving 'in close attendance on the First Consul' (and Emperor) – that is, each day's duty squadron and escort piquet. This feature of the *tenue en service près du premier consul* is not generally known. The figure also shows the *aurore* tape and scarlet piping that decorated the troopers' dark green portmanteau and shabraque, and the *aurore*-on-scarlet corner ornament – which copied the turnback ornament on the men's long-tailed *habit* coats worn in *tenue ordinaire*.

## B3: Trumpeter, Consular Guard; uniform for service in attendance on the First Consul, 1803–04
The 1802 reorganization raised the number of trumpeters to three per company, the 12 in the regiment being led by a trumpet-major and two trumpet-corporals. The substitution of sky-blue and crimson with gold-and-crimson lace, cords and barrel-sash for the regimental uniform colours followed the common practice for trumpeters throughout the Guard cavalry. Again, he wears the deerskin breeches. The peaked (visored) version of the trumpeters' white colback was only worn briefly in about 1803.

## C1 & C2: Chasseurs, Imperial Guard; uniform for service in attendance on the Emperor, 1804–15
Each day, the duty squadron of the regiment had to provide an escort piquet for Napoleon; this was described in the memoirs of Capt Parquin as follows: 'A total of one lieu-

A trooper of the Mounted Chasseurs in winter Sunday walking-out dress of scarlet pelisse and green full-dress breeches with the bicorn hat. When the pelisse made its first appearance in c.1800 it had three rows of buttons, but five rows were introduced from 1803 onwards; normally it was only closed by means of the top few buttons, spreading open below the mid-chest. The bicorn, a remnant of the Guides' campaign dress before and during the Egyptian campaign, is dressed here with the red-over-green plume, large tricolour cockade, and loop and ties in *aurore*. (Army Museum, Brussels)

tenant, one sergeant *[maréchal-des-logis]*, two corporals *[brigadiers]*, 22 troopers and a trumpeter formed the Emperor's party. The Emperor had but to stop or put a foot on the ground and the Chasseurs did likewise, fixed bayonets on their musketoons, and proceeded in square, the Emperor at the centre. The commanding officer of this escort was invariably by his Majesty's side, and only King Murat or the Prince of Neuchatel [Marshal Berthier, the chief-of-staff] had the right to come between them.'

Generally the commentaries to B1 and B2 also apply here, with the obvious difference of the substitution of Imperial insignia – i.e. the crowned eagle – for Consular. Note that this also appears in miniature on the white-red-blue cockade at the base of the plume. The larger size of the colback in fact dates these figures to post-1806. A bayonet has now been issued for the musketoon, its frog stitched to the left side of the sword belt behind the first suspension ring. The front of the shabraque covered two holstered saddle pistols.

**C3: Chasseur, Imperial Guard, grande tenue ordinaire**
This has been described, erroneously, as a 'No.2 dress' uniform; in fact it was an alternative full dress, as worn by those squadrons other than that which was serving as daily duty squadron. The *habit*, recalling the old Guides, has scarlet collar, cuffs and piping; *aurore* aiguillettes and right shoulder knot; and *aurore*-on-scarlet bugle-horn ornaments on the turnbacks. It is worn over a scarlet waistcoat, now with a single row of buttons and *aurore* braiding (see H2 for the braiding style). The dark green breeches have the same decorations as B1's scarlet version. This figure's mount would have the same horse furniture as in C1.

**D/E: GENERAL RAPP AT AUSTERLITZ, 2 DECEMBER 1805**
After leading two unsuccessful charges by squadrons from the cavalry of the French Imperial Guard against those of the Russian Imperial Guard, Napoleon's ADC **General Rapp (1)** leads the duty squadron of the Mounted Chasseurs in a third attempt, which will prove irresistible – though Rapp himself will soon suffer a serious face wound. He is followed by a trumpeter of the duty squadron, in sky-blue with deerskin breeches and a white colback; and he is flanked by two aides, distinguished by their dark blue uniforms faced sky-blue and the red-and-gold brassards of ADCs to a divisional general. At Austerlitz the Mounted Chasseurs fought in their pelisses; the **squadron-leader (2)** has the handsome version purchased by officers, with gold lace and cords and white fur trim – note also his expensive green leather pouch and belt trimmed with gold. The Chasseurs hit the disordered formations of the **Chevalier Guards; (3) and (4)** are an officer and trooper of that regiment which, with the Horse Guards, suffered severe casualties at Austerlitz. At right, a **Russian Guard Horse Artillery gunner (5)**, from the battery that the Chasseurs had already overrun, tries to escape from the cavalry mêlée.

**F1: Officer, grande tenue de parade, 1810–15**
The rank was indicated by lace *en pique* on the thighs of the breeches and on the sleeves of the dolman; all officers wore a single inner lace, and the other three here identify a captain company commander. The extremely expensive privately purchased uniforms and equipment of officers, in fine cloth and leather positively encrusted with gold bullion lace, often showed minor individual variations. This parade full dress uniform is essentially that worn since the beginning of the Empire, but two features are notable: the very long hussar boots, almost touching the kneecap, were fashionable in about 1810–12; and the slinging of the pelisse to hang low over the arm was also an affectation which became popular during the later Empire.

**F2: Officer, grande tenue ordinaire, 1805–15**
See commentary to C3, which applies equally here, except that the officer has all gold distinctions, and wears the appropriate epaulette of rank on the *habit*.

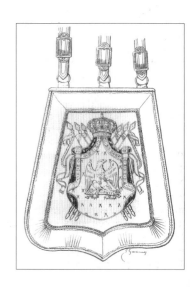

The Mounted Chasseurs used several types of sabretache, from this colourful and finely embroidered quality to a plain black version with a central crowned eagle in brass. They were the only unit to display these full Imperial arms.

**F3: Officer, Imperial escort piquet, 1810–15**
Parade full dress is worn with the deerskin breeches. The saddle cover of false panther-skin is typical for officers; and the second-quality sabretache, less expensive for field use, is taken from the *Cahiers de la Malmaison* regulations.

**F4: Senior officer, winter full dress, 1804–15**
The white plume indicates a member of the regimental staff.

**G1: Chasseur, duty squadron, *tenue de campagne*, 1805–15**
For this duty he wears a fully dressed colback. The use of the pelisse as a jacket in cold weather was both sensible and popular; but for a year after the Austerlitz campaign it would generally only be available to officers, who bought their own. Pelisses were worn by all ranks during the 1805 campaign, but sustained so much damage, and were so costly to replace, that they were not taken into the field in 1806–07 – when they must have been sorely missed in the bitter Polish winter. He has his cloak rolled and tied around his torso as protection from sabre cuts. His breeches are protected by side-buttoned overalls with leather booting, and his sabretache by a black waxed cloth cover; the rear corners of the shabraque are hooked up to protect the embroidered ornaments from dirt and damage on the march and in battle.

**G2: Chasseur, *tenue de campagne, service ordinaire*, 1805–15**
This trooper, whose squadron is not on duty in attendance on the Emperor, wears the field order of the *service ordinaire* uniform – see C3. The bearskin colback is stripped of its plume and cords, and the *flamme* is folded and concealed on the top under a hooked-on black leather crown cover. Under the *habit* the old undecorated scarlet waistcoat with two rows of buttons – *gilet rond* – is worn instead of the fancier version with *aurore* braiding. Again, the breeches are protected by overalls (*'charivari'*), of which a number of variations have been illustrated after c.1808: with double *aurore* stripes replacing the wide scarlet stripe; the same, but without buttons and with doubled green cloth replacing the leather booting; grey, with leather booting and two red stripes; and – after the First Restoration – of green with black booting and a single red stripe.

**G3: Officer, summer field dress, c.1812**
Like their men, officers not in attendance on Napoleon laid aside all superfluous (and expensive to replace) decorative features when they were on campaign, in favour of convenience and relative simplicity. The bearskin is not dressed; the dolman is worn alone, without the pelisse (which was seldom seen in the field after c.1809); and the pouchbelt is shrouded in a buttoned leather cover. Officers, too, wore overalls, but here these are replaced by simpler plain green trousers with gold sidestripes; these would have a doubling of green cloth to do the job of the leather booting.

**H1: Mounted kettle-drummer, c.1804–05**
This mounted drummer led the regiment on the day of Napoleon's coronation in December 1804, when the weather was distinctly cold for such a light outfit – it was the fashion of the time to dress these young musicians in fanciful oriental costumes. The illustration is copied from a Hoffmann plate (see above).

**H2: Trumpet-major, *seconde tenue de parade***
This order of dress, with its cutaway *habit* and exposed

Entering the Consular Guard at the age of 14, Bruno Lemoine was of such small stature that in 1804 the artist Hoffmann thought he was still a child. As the regimental kettle-drummer he wears the then-fashionable Mameluke style of uniform and headdress (see Plate H1); the most eye-catching items are the richly embroidered drum banners, showing the Imperial arms among palm branches. The horse's headstall is ornamented with tricolour plumes, and the gold-on-green saddle cloth shows bugle-horns above palms in the rear corners. (Ann S.K. Brown Collection, Providence, USA)

waistcoat, echoes that of the trooper in C3. The sky-blue worn by trumpeters instead of dark green includes the plume of his bearskin. The gold-and-crimson trumpeters' lace is seen in the braiding of his crimson waistcoat – the *gilet à la hussarde* – and the embroidered Hungarian knots and sidestripes on his breeches; the aiguillette and trumpet cord are in the same colours. His rank is indicated by the gold double chevrons above his gold-trimmed cuffs, the double edging of his lapels, and the triple edging of his collar.

**H3: Trumpeter, duty squadron, parade full dress**
Like the officers and the other rankers, for this order of dress the trumpeters wore the hussar-style uniform of dolman and pelisse in their distinctive sky-blue, crimson and gold, with the white colback. Once again, the deerskin breeches identify the duty squadron, serving close to the Emperor's tented 'household' and General Headquarters in the field.

# INDEX

Figures in **bold** refer to illustrations.

Aboukir Bay, battle of (1798) 6
Allimant, Lt 42
Arcole, battle of (1796) 4–5
Aspern/Essling, battle of (1809) 24
Augereau, Marshal Pierre (1757–1816) 17
Austerlitz, battle of (1805) 13–15
    aftermath 15–16
Austrian forces 4–5, 12–13, 15, 39

Bagration, Gen Prince Pyotr
    (1765–1812) 14
Bassano, battle of (1796) 4
Beauharnais, Eugène de (1781–1824)
    6, **6**, 7, **8**, 9, 10, **11**, **12**, **13**, **14**, 15, 19
Bennigsen, Count von Levin (1745–1826)
    17, 19, 40
Berthier, Marshal Louis-Alexandre
    (1733–1815) 5, 10, 33
Bessières, Marshal Jean-Baptiste
    (1768–1813) 4–5, 6, 7, 9, 12, 13, 14,
    20, 23, 35, 38
Blücher, Gen Gebhard von (1714–1819)
    43, 44
Bonaparte, Joseph (1768–1844) 21
Brice, Lt 39
British forces 43

Charles, Archduke, of Austria
    (1771–1847) 24, 33
Confederation of the Rhine 16
Constantine, Grand Duke Pavlovich
    (1779–1831) 14
Consular Guard 7–9 see also Imperial
    Guard; Mounted Chasseurs

Dahlmann, Gen Nicolas (1769–1807) 7,
    9, 14, **14**, 15, 16, 17, 18
Davout, Marshal Louis Nicolas
    (1770–1823) 17, 18
Desmichel, Capt 12–13
Domingue, Capt Joseph 'Hercule' 5, 8,
    9, 33
Douai, Gen Merlin de (1754–1838) 43
Duroc, Gen Geraud (1772–1813) 37
Dutch forces 43

Egyptian campaign 5–7
equipment 16–17
Eylau, battle of (1807) 17

Ferdinand Karl Joseph, Archduke of
    Austria (1781–1850) 12–13
Fourth Coalition 16
France, campaign of (1814) 41–43
Friedland, battle of (1807) 19

German campaign (1813) 39–41
German forces 40–41, 43
Gutschenreiter, Lt Jean-Baptiste
    (1782–1859) **34**
Guyot, Gen (b.1768) 15, 16, 20, 21, **22**,
    23, 24, 33, 34, 35, 36, 37, 38, 39

Hannau, battle of (1813) 40–41
'Hercule' see Domingue, Capt Joseph
    'Hercule'

Imperial Guard 9–11, 15, 38–39 see also
    Consular Guard; Mounted Chasseurs
    establishment 10–11, 21, 34, 35, 37–39
    New Guard 38–39
    numbers hospitalized (1810) 35

Old Guard 38–39
Vélites 11, 16, 34
Italian campaigns
    (1796–97) 4–5
    (1800–01) 7
John, Archduke, of Austria 24, 33
Junot, Gen Andoche (1771–1813) 4

Kellermann, Gen François (1735–1820) 3
Kléber, Gen Jean (1753–1800) 6
Krettly, Trumpet-Maj 14, 15, 17, 42
Kutuzov, Marshal Mikhail (1745–1813)
    13, 14

Lannes, Marshal Jean (1769–1809) 4,
    14, 19
Lefebvre-Desnoëttes, Gen Count Charles
    (1773–1822) 20, 21, 22, 23, 24, 36, 37,
    38, 39, 42, 43, 44
Leipzig, battle of (1813) 39–40
Ligny, battle of (1815) 44
Lion, Gen 42, 43
Lonato, battle of (1796) 4
Louis XVIII, King of France
    (1755–1824) 43

Mack, Gen Karl von (1752–1828) 12
Madrid city riots (1808) 20–21
Marengo, battle of (1800) 7
Mamelukes 9, 10, 11, 14, 17, 20, 21, 22,
    34, 35, 36
monarchy, restoration of (1814) 43
Moore, Sir John (1761–1809) 21–22, 23
Morland, Col 9, 10, 14
Mount Tabor, battle of (1799) 6
Mounted Chasseurs see also Consular
    Guard; Imperial Guard
    expansion and numbers of 4–5, 15–16,
        20, 35, 36
    Officers' Roll 41
    origins of 3–4
    rebuilding of (1813) 37–39, 41–42
Murat, Marshal Joachim (1767–1815) 4,
    12, 13, 14, 17, 20

Nansouty, Gen Etienne (1768–1815) 41
Napoleon Bonaparte (1769–1821) **24**, **42**
    at Austerlitz 13, 14
    and Austria 23
    and Consular Guard 7
    and Consulate regime 7
    and Egypt 5–7
    at Eylau 17, 18
    and first surrender 42–43
    and The Hundred Days 43–44
    and Imperial Guard 9
    and origins of Mounted Chasseurs 3–4
    and Prussia 16
    and Russia 37
    and Spanish campaign 21, 22, 23
    and Wagram 33
Nelson, Adm Horatio (1758–1805) 6
Ney, Marshal Michel (1769–1815) 17,
    18, 44
Nile, battle of (1798) 6

Oudinot, Capt 40, 41

Paget, LtGen Henry 22, 23
Parquin, Lt Denis-Charles 40, **40**, 41
Pleswitz armistice (1813) 39
Polish campaign (1806) 16–17
Pressburg, Treaty of (1805) 15
Prussian campaign (1806) 16

Prussian forces 43, 44

Rapp, Gen Jean (1771–1821) 14
    at Austerlitz (1805) **D**, **E**, (28–29, 46)
Repnin, Prince 14
Rovereto, battle of (1796) 4
Russian campaign (1812) 35–37
Russian forces 13, 14, 15, 40

sebretaches **46**
Soult, Marshal Nicolas (1769–1851) 14,
    21, 23
Spanish campaigns
    (1807–08) 20–23
    (1810–12) 34–35
Swedish forces 40

Talleyrand, Charles de (1754–1838)
    18
Third Coalition 15
Thomas, Capt Hypolite 3, **3**
Tilsit, Treaty of (1807) 19
Turkish forces 6

Ulm, battle of (1805) 12–13
uniforms **3**, **4**, **8**, 9, 10, **10**, **11**, **12**, **13**, **14**,
    **15**, **16**, **19**, **20**, **21**, **22**, **24**, **33**, **34**, **37**, **38**,
    **40**, **44**, **45**, **46**, **47**
Consular Guard (1803–04)
    Chasseurs **B1**, **B2**, (26, 45)
    Trumpeter **B3**, (26, 45)
Guide de Bonaparte
    Egypt (1798–99) **A2** (25, 45);
        Officer **A3** (25, 45)
    Italy (1796–97) **A1** (25, 45)
Imperial Guard
    (1804–05)
        Mounted kettle-drummer **H1**
            (32, 47)
    (1804–15)
        Chasseurs **C** (27, 45–46)
        at Austerlitz (1805) **D**, **E**
            (28–29, 46)
        Officer winter full dress **F4** (30,
            47)
    (1805–15)
        Chasseur duty squadron tenue de
            campagne **G1** (31, 47)
        Chasseur tenue de campaign service
            ordinaire **G2** (31, 47)
        Officer grande tenue ordinaire **F2**
            (30, 46)
    (1810–15)
        Officer escort piquet **F3** (30, 47)
        Officer grande tenue de parade **F1**
            (30, 46)
    (1812)
        Officer summer field dress **G3**
            (31, 47)
        Trumpet-Major seconde tenue de
            parade **H2** (32, 47)
        Trumpeter duty squadron parade
            full dress **H3** (32, 47)
Napoleon **24**, **42**
Gen Rapp at Austerlitz (1805) **D**, **E**
    (28–29, 46)

Vélites 11, 16, 34

Wagram, battle of (1809) 24, 33–34
Waterloo, battle of (1815) 44
Wellesley, Arthur, Duke of Wellington
    (1769–1852) 21, 43
Wrede, Gen Karl von (1767–1838) 40, 41